Duong Le Quy:
The First Play Collection

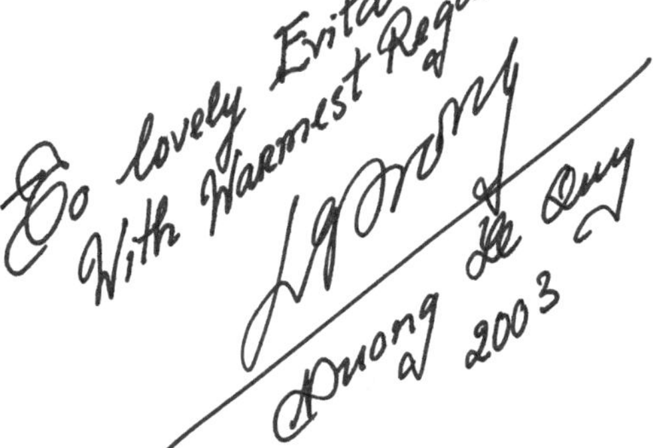

Currency Press • Sydney

CURRENCY PLAYS

First published 2002,
Currency Press Pty Ltd,
PO Box 2287, Strawberry Hills, NSW, 2012, Australia
enquiries@currency.com.au
www.currency.com.au

Market of Lives first published in *Young Playwrights: Eleven New Plays* (ed. Errol Bray) by Currency Press, 1994; *Meat Party* first published by Currency Press, 2000.

NATIONAL LIBRARY OF AUSTRALIA CIP DATA
    Duong Le Quy, 1968–.
       [Plays. Selelctions]
       The first play collection.
       ISBN 0 86819 684 3.
       I. Title.
    A822.3

Set by Dean Nottle
Printed by Hyde Park Press, Richmond, South Australia
Cover design by Tony Yap

CONTENTS

Duong Le Quy: The First Play Collection

There were days which were not the same as a thousand other days

Poem by Duong Le Quy
Translation by Lien Yeomans

There were days which were not the same as a thousand other days,
days when bombs in thousands rained down around me
days when people in thousands went away never to return.

There were days which were not the same as a thousand other days,
days when I was lost along roads dressed in the white of mourning
    gowns
amongst ruined houses,
amongst crowded markets where people strove to escape the silent
    cries.

War!

There were days which were not the same as a thousand other days,
when tears fell and washed the palms of hands,
when cold afternoon light fell on the back of the blind soldier
    returning with uncertain step,
seeking his lover who had become one of the mists of smoke
when chants calling back dead souls could be heard from rows of
    crude earth graves.

War!

Guns, bombs went past
leaving behind different shapes on my country
leaving behind different beats in the hearts of my people
leaving behind memories of days which were not the same as a
    thousand other days

Introduction

Katharine Brisbane

'The past! The past made bitter and sad by your deception', says the blind man Trung in *Market of Lives*.

'You can never bury the past', sings the Chorus.

'How can we go to the future if we don't know the past?', asks Con in *A Graveyard for the Living*.

'Killing people is easy. To be able to live after the killing is much more difficult', observes Mr Thé.

The past, the so recent past, dominates Duong Le Quy's writing in these three plays, together with its damaged minds and bodies and the beautiful, desecrated landscape of his native home. The plays are set in the 1980s, in the aftermath of the American War, as the Vietnamese call it—a time when many secrets were uncovered in the process of reform and reconstruction. And yet, while *Meat Party* does tangentially deal with Australia's contribution to that war, the plays are not essentially about the impact of external forces on his crippled country but on the internal forces of class wars, the pain of traditional values destroyed. Ho Chi Min's Spartan presence looms over the play, the spirit gone, the rulebook remaining in the hands of old men. Quan, a local bureaucrat in *Meat Party* puts his finger on the dilemma of conflicting allegiances:

> Father, I have to face thousands of problems… I carry on my shoulder the responsibilities for a better future of the entire population in this region. I have no time to concern myself with one crazy old man… Providing a house for a person who dishonoured you? In my opinion Socialism has no room for such a person!

To which his father replies: 'Your duty is to help people like him to change—spiritually and physically—even if it costs you your life.' (p.63)

Anyone who has visited Vietnam cannot fail to be aware that communism is—or was—a religion as much as an ideology and had more than its share of martyrs. In Le Quy's plays its control over moral values has descended into corruption, nepotism and revenge. All three plays are a plea for confession, for the restoration of old community loyalties and for the expiation of past actions. It is a timely message for Australia, itself struggling with exposure of its own ugly past while at the same time raising further barriers to human happiness for new waves of future citizens. Duong Le Quy's plays stand as an awful warning of the consequences, not of war itself but of the cancers that eat at the roots of a society damaged by exploitation and fear.

In *Market of Lives* the village market is to be demolished to make way for a more modern one. Trung, an old blind man, whose apparent prophetic voice derives from knowing too much and living too long, inhabits the market, along with Thanh, a young man, driven mad by the war, who sings endlessly about a better world. A young newspaper seller barks like a dog to attract more customers. Tran Cong, a member of the City People's Committee, is seen by his biographer Tu Du as 'a shining example of a devoted cadre'. When he goes to inspect the market he encounters Trung and is confronted with his long-buried past. This haunting past is common to all three plays and assumes in *Meat Party* Macbeth-like overtones as Lam, the revered war hero, is pursued by the ghosts of dead souls. They rise, too, in the White Sand Desert as Mary, an Australian musician, searches for the grave of her soldier father in *Meat Party*. They have keepers in the mad old Crone, and the old soldier An, who watch over the bones of the desert; and in the scarred Mrs Dat and her mad companion Old Son in *A Graveyard for the Living*.

The mad, here, are the thinkers. An tells Mary, 'My poems are of no use to the Proletarian Revolution of the White Sand Desert... To understand is to remember. To remember is to think! And to think is to want to change what has been understood.' Thinking is subversive. Once one has thought there is no going back. The old hero Lam, like Cong, has buried the spirit of reform with his early acts of betrayal but continues to train his son in the disciplines of correctness. His son is preoccupied with the ways forward but keeps from his father news of the fall of the Soviet Union for fear of hurting him. Another deceit. When Mary unwittingly refers to this, Lam's fabricated world dissolves into dust.

A Graveyard for the Living is the angriest of the three plays. It deals with the legacy of the Land Reform Movement of 1954, in which the peasants rose up against the landowner, and the war against the colonising French that followed. The play is set on a peninsular of land reclaimed to bury the thousands of landowning families who died during this revolt. The old couple Mrs Dat and Old Son are survivors of that massacre; Con, Mrs Dat's cadre son, and Mr Thé, his boss, hero of the battle of Dien Bien Phu, are woven into the story also. Thé wants the land for apartment blocks and his plans finally confront him with the effects of his merciless regime and its origins in the revenge he took for his treatment at the hands of the landowners. Both sides were guilty and in the anarchy that followed both sides suffered.

The style of the plays is poetic; Australian senses could mistake them for folk tales. They are full of images of peasant life, of glowing sunsets and desert plains. A singer is central to the emotional thread, commenting mournfully upon the action. The sun is like blood or fire, the darkness is fearful. Dead souls haunt the protagonists; *A Graveyard for the Living* is Gothic in its extravagance. But do not be deceived by this exoticism. The plays are dealing with real history, a history that has left a whole nation on intimate terms with atrocity. Any visitor to Vietnam cannot fail to be aware, in the surviving evidence of the wars, of extremities of suffering and revenge and anger at the heart. Nor can he or she fail to recognise the controls with which officialdom seeks to keep the nation smiling. 'You have to know how to show off the good and hide the bad', says To, sprucing up the market for the cadre's inspection at the opening of *Market of Lives*. And again in Scene Four as Tu Du is airing heroic phrases for his biography of the war hero Cong, Cong's wife Phuong remarks: 'Don't you think that's a little strong?' 'Oh yes, but leave it like that', Tu Du replies, 'the editorial board will tone it down.' That is, the government's, not the publisher's, editorial board. Censorship is everywhere.

There is also hope. The old cadres recognise at last the hollowness of their ideology and the need for change, though they are powerless to initiate it. The old people come to terms with their losses. And as the past reveals itself the young people begin to shed the burdens it imposed. In *Market of Lives* the market is restored. In *Meat Party* the war is laid to rest with the body of Mary's father, fused forever with that of the Vietnamese nurse who showed him compassion. In *Graveyard* the dead souls rest and the river flows on.

Duong Le Quy is too young to remember the American War. But he grew up with the consequences. He graduated from the Hanoi Institute of Theatre and Cinema in 1990 and began writing poetry and plays before coming to Australia in 1994 to learn English. In this he was encouraged by his parents, who saw the deleterious effect of political correctness on creativity. The same year his play *Market of Lives* received a workshop at InterPlay, the international young playwrights' organisation in Townsville. Encouragement from the arts community persuaded him to apply to immigrate under the special skills category and in 1999 he became an Australian citizen.

Since coming to Australia he has been indefatigable—and remarkably successful—in seeking a better understanding between people of his two countries. In this he has seen the arts as outriders and has arranged many exchange visits through his organisation VACEP, the Vietnamese-Australian Cultural Exchange Program. Censorship on one side and conservatism on the other impede his progress but his many awards in Australia are tribute to the message he brings and the skill and passion with which he expresses it. He has now embarked upon a new trilogy addressing contemporary Australia. We can expect that a critique of his new country will be as uncompromising as that of his old.

Sydney
June 2002

Writer's Note

I have long held the desire to have this collection of my plays about Vietnam published. Each play looks at the country from a different perspective and can be likened to another eye opening. And each eye looks onto an ocean of red—the colour of blood. Vietnam is bathed in the blood of war and of sorrow. But red also represents the sun and I see the people of Vietnam full of hopes and dreams. And it is the colour of roses, for the Vietnam I know is full of love and a faithfulness as strong as any lover.

It is my great pleasure to present to you my first play collection. I have included three plays: *Market of Lives* (produced by Wollongong University/Theatre South in 1998); *Meat Party* (produced by Playbox/Melbourne International Arts Festival in 2000); and *A Graveyard for the Living* (introduced by the Australian Script Centre in its 2001 collection).

In offering these plays, I also offer a prayer to the souls of all those innocent people who have suffered injustice, unnecessary pain and misery, and have died in all the wars on this earth. I hope that they will be reborn into a better world where ignorance and lies no longer prevail and that these tragedies are never repeated. I also hope for a new future in Vietnam of peace and happiness.

Today's world is rapidly changing, and I feel deeply inside my writer's heart that it is time for the many innocent dead to be reborn. I want to write about them and their secret world. Yes! There is a secret world peopled by all the souls who have ever lived whose whispers to us—Human Beings—are that we never need to be born or to die meaninglessly.

As those many human souls visit every corner of our planet they ask the questions: Why do the innocent have to die and what will humans do to preserve a future free of war, disease and sorrow? The more we discuss these questions, the more enlightened we become and, ultimately, the less we need to ask the questions. It is my wish that this collection—my modest contribution to this discussion—will take you on a quiet journey into the spiritual world of these souls and their desire to seek answers to these questions.

Whenever I complete a play I feel enormous relief. But that relief is accompanied by the great happiness one can find in living a life not only for the present, but also for the past and the future. The past might be full of war and sorrow, the present might be full of confusion and difficulties, but we can fill the future with love and hope. It helps us make sense of our existence. It allows us to perceive our existence not only in its everyday physical form, but with the knowledge that we are being watched over by the invisible world.

Like all playwrights, I hope that my plays will have many directors who will take many different approaches. Although these productions will all be different, I trust that these texts, in their published form, will continue to tell the stories in my original voice. It is my wish that my humble works may go some way towards creating a world in which we human beings will soon begin to live together in peace, progress and happiness.

Duong Le Quy
Melbourne
June 2002

ACKNOWLEDGEMENTS

First of all, I would like to express my deepest gratitude to my parents who never stop encouraging me to work in the arts. My sincere thanks also go to Mr Le Anh Linh and Ms Lien Yeomans who have worked extremely hard to translate these plays from the original Vietnamese into English. I cannot thank enough to the following colleagues who wrote letters to support my application for residence in Australia in 1994: Dr Errol Bray, Bruce Keller, Elian Morel, Dave Brown, Christopher Wynton, Stephen Champion, Roland Manderson, Keith Gallasch and Virginia Baxter, Chris Johnston, Victoria Jones, Robyn Kershaw, Kim Hanna, the late Sandra Gorman, Mike Canfield, Cheryle Yin-Lo, Michael FitzGerald and Sue Elmes.

I would also like to take this opportunity to express my deep gratitude to the following Australian arts individuals for their continued heartfelt encouragement for my work: John Romeril, Carillo Gartner, May-Brit Akerholt, Aubrey Mellor, Ann Tonks, Jill Smith, Sue McCreadie, Campion Decent, David Wilmoth, Christopher McGill, Elizabeth Butcher, Chris Gallagher, Susan Strano, Amanda Lawrence, Jose Borghino, Mary-Anne Gifford, Lex Marinos, Stephen Sewell, Peter Matheson, Angela Chaplin, Geoff Crowhurst, Brett Johnson, Susan Donnely, Douglas Horton, Ken Healy, Sue Rider, Gordon Beattie, Vanessa Pigrum, Martin Croft, Hung Tran, Chris Mead, Don Reid, Liberty Kerr, Keith Robinson, Fiona Press, Rachel Hennessy, the late David Branson, Yaron Lifschitz, Jim Cotter, Anni Davey, Arne Sjostedt, Michael Kantor, Matthew Crosby, Alice Garner, Yumi Umiumare, Huong Nguyen, Tam Phan, Darrin Verhagen, Ursula Yovich, Miki Oikawa, Justin Cheek, Bradley Byquar, Andrew Livingston & Ben Cobham, Trang Nguyen, Janys Hayes, Kate Donelan, Dorotka Sapinska, Donna Hewitt, Marian Abboud, John-Paul Hussey, Simon Kingsley, Mary Rachel Brown, Helen Thomson, Larissa Dubecki, Robin Usher, Celia Kennedy, Pamela Payne, Katrina Strickland, Suzanne Brown, Neil Litchfield, Jo Litson and the many other people whose support will stay in my memory forever.

My special thanks and deep gratitude go to Dr Katharine Brisbane, Victoria Chance, Nick Parsons, Dean Nottle, Claire Grady, Deborah Franco, Margaret Leask and everyone at Currency Press for their time, energy and highly professional support which enabled this publication to see the light of day. I must also express my utmost admiration and thanks to all of my friends and colleagues at Playbox Theatre for their continued invaluable support. I consider myself privileged to have my play *Meat Party* presented by such a dynamic and creative company. I also would like to thank Tony Yap for his wonderful cover design, along with the many other individuals and companies who have helped bring this collection to its readers.

May I express my deep thanks and appreciation to the support of the following arts organisations: Australia Council for the Arts, NSW Ministry for the Arts, Arts Victoria, Australian Society of Authors, Australian Writers' Guild, Churchill Memorial Trust, Asialink, Australian—American Fulbright Commission, NIDA, School of Theatre and Film Studies—UNSW, Melbourne International Festival, Melbourne Fringe Festival, Carnivale Festival, Chamber Made Opera, Melbourne Theatre Company, Belvoir Street Theatre, Playbox Theatre, Queensland Government—Premier's Literary Awards, Queensland Theatre Company, Australian National Playwrights' Centre, Wollongong University, Melbourne University, RMIT, Drama Victoria, Performance Space, National Book Council, Centre for Performance Studies, Playworks and the many other organisations which have always encouraged my work.

In Vietnam, mothers tell their children that: 'When eating a fruit, think of the person who planted the tree'. This play collection is a small fruit in the very rich garden of Australian playwriting, Please accept my gratitude to you all—the individuals and the organisations— who have planted the tree since the time I first came to Australia. Forgive me if I have not included your name in this acknowledgment. The page is limited but your support is not—it is unforgettable and immeasurable. That support will be in my heart wherever I go because without it my works may well have remained buried within and never grown to bear fruit.

Duong Le Quy
Melbourne
June 2002

Market of Lives

(Cho Doi)

Translation by Le Anh Linh

Translation edited by Eliane Anh-Xuan Morel
and Janys Hayes

For my mother, and all my good friends.

CHARACTERS

TRUNG, blind war veteran who sells Dong ho pictures (Vietnamese traditional pictures) at the markets

TRAN CONG, cadre of the city

PHUONG, Tran Cong's wife

SONG ANH, Tran Cong and Phuong's daughter, a student at the teachers' training college

TU DU, Song Anh's boyfriend, also a student at the teachers' training college

THANH, an invalid war veteran

LE, Thanh's girlfriend, a cleaner in the market

TO, market manager

MRS NGA, seller of herbal medicines in the markets

TOM, Mrs Nga's son, newpaper seller

THIET, Tran Cong's secretary

SCENE ONE

A shabby and muddy market. Very early morning. Everything seems to be still sleeping. MRS NGA *is taking out the winnowing basket of cigarettes.* MR TRUNG *is making traditional Dong ho pictures with his sense of touch.* THANH *is staggering about, as if still asleep. In the distance,* LE *is sweeping. Suddenly some gamblers are heard quarrelling loudly.*

TO: [*whistling as he enters the market*] Who? Who? Who's gambling so early in the morning? Who's picking a fight? Why are you making the market so noisy?

GAMBLER: Good morning! This is only a friendly meeting. We've only come down here to get meat for our children, that's all.

TO: [*smiling*] Oh! I see! But you know that you must be pleasant to each other when you get together, be friendly…

GAMBLER: … helping and sharing with each other.

TO: That is right. Remember this is a market.

NGA: It must have order, discipline and regulations.

TO: Shut up! You've just been allowed into this market. Don't interrupt me! If you keep interrupting me like that you've got to go somewhere else to earn your living. Understand?

> TRUNG *enters.*

LE: Good morning, Mr Trung. Why are you here so early today??

TRUNG: I've been listening to the happy sounds of the market. I've been listening to To singing as happily as a bird, not grumbling, like he usually does.

TO: You're blind, it heightens your other senses. Your hearing's so good you can even hear the very market breathing.

TRUNG: I was born here, grew up here. There used to be a river here. Gradually the river silted up and eventually became the village and then the city and the markets. [*To* TO] So, tell us, what makes you so happy? Tell everybody, please!

TO: Listen, listen everybody! Listen carefully! Today, everyone must be well-dressed.

GAMBLERS: Well-dressed?

TO: Yes, well-dressed!

GAMBLER 1: My shirt's okay, but my trousers have some patches.

GAMBLER 2: My trousers don't have any patches but my shirt's torn.

TO: Hmm! You have to know how to show off the good, and hide the bad! You two exchange clothes! The one with the good shirt sits in front. The one with the patched trousers stands behind. Is that clear?

GAMBLERS: Yes, that's clear.

TRUNG: What are you hiding, Mr To?

TO: Today there is a cadre coming to visit the market. It will be wonderful!

NGA: Oh, Budda! Another cadre! What'll they do this time? Increase our taxes again, or inspect our trade licences, or—

TO: No, no, something much more significant. He is coming here to conduct a survey for the preparation of a new market!

TRUNG: You mean a new market will replace the old one?

TO: Yes, that's right! This muddy, shabby old market, littered with bomb craters, will be flattened and a nice new one built.

NGA: Bigger and more beautiful.

TO: Exactly, but you're interrupting me again!

LE: Dear Mr To! That's great news! A new market! Is this really true?

GAMBLERS: Is this really true?

TO: Yes, this time it's true. So, let's get motivated. We must implement a plan of action. Now, let's get down to details… Mrs Nga and the herbalists will take the rubbish from the sewers on the left. Mr Xom and the [dog meat] butchers will clear the sewers and the bomb craters on the right. Miss Le and the grocers and the cyclo drivers will do the sewers and the bomb craters out the back. My son will direct the group of rice sellers to clear the drains and the bomb craters in the front. Is that clear?

GAMBLERS: Yes. That's clear.

TO: All right! Off you go! Do what I've told you.

The CHORUS *exit.*

TRUNG: What! Sewers and bomb craters on all four sides! So many years have gone by and we're still surrounded by sewerage and bomb craters?

TO: Nothing changes, Mr Trung. Your eyes are damaged, you can't see the filth, so you believe that everything around is clean and changed.

NGA: Oh, Mr Trung! Don't be sad, it won't do you any good.

THANH: [*getting up with his guitar*] Artist Thanh greets the sky, greets the land and greets myself…

LE: [*rushing to hold* THANH] Thanh! I am here! Don't do that! Everyone's preparing to build a new market!

THANH: [*singing*] 'Ah my country, my country, my country… Building sites in the yellow sunlight. Building sites, nice with lots of hope, la la la…'

TO: Heaven and Earth! The madman! How can we make him come to his senses?

THANH: [*singing*] 'One lives with the other for love, for today, for tomorrow, for many following generations…'

NGA: What a pity. He's losing himself again. Le! Here, take some herb leaves for him to chew, see if that'll do him any good.

TRUNG: He may well be the happiest person in the market. He sounds very happy when he's singing.

LE: Oh, Trung! What am I to do with him now?

TRUNG: Let him sing. He's like me. We'd rather see nothing and understand nothing.

LE: No! Mr Trung, Mr To, Mrs Nga, please, try to explain to him what's really happening. The songs he's singing are pointless. Thanh! You have to live in reality even if it is sad. You can't live in your dreams! Thanh…

THANH: [*singing*] 'For today, for tomorrow, for many generations…'

TO: Thanh! Do you recognise me? It's me, To! Market Manager!

THANH: Stand up straight! Artist Thanh greets Artist Vo Van To.

LE: [*crying*] Oh, Thanh! Sleep, my darling. The people in the market have collected some money for you. I'll take you to hospital.

THANH: Hospital! [*Slapping* LE*'s cheek, singing*] 'Do you still remember the makeshift hospital at the front where many of my comrades closed their eyes for ever…'

TO: What a terrible business! Terrible business! When the cadre comes, what will he think of us if he sees Thanh carrying on like this? Whoever Thanh meets, he calls 'Great Artist'!

THANH: When thinking of a life, I remember a forest. When thinking of a forest, I suddenly remember many other people… [*Singing*] 'Oh, my country, my country… The burned-out forests left by the bombs…'

TO: Oh, Thanh! Please, please, I beg you, be quiet. The cadre is coming!

THANH *continues singing then falls asleep.*

Yes, yes, that's right, keep sleeping. Have a good nap. Sleep all day long if you like. When there is a new market you will be able to sing to your heart's content.

LE: Sleep, my darling! You will be happy in your dreams.

NGA: Oh, Buddha! Miss Le, Mr Trung is drawing a picture of you! Mr Trung! How do you do that?

TRUNG: I hear the voice and know what the person looks like! Le's voice, it's warm, just like the earth… Mr To! Don't let anyone walk on this picture I've drawn of Le!

TO: You know, rain will come and the water will wash it away. Say, Trung, were you ever a painter?

TRUNG: Long ago. A very long time ago. Perhaps if the war hadn't deprived me of my vision.

TO: You're a war invalid. Why don't you live in the war invalid's camp? How can you improve your life painting pictures in this market?

TRUNG: You'd never understand.

Someone laughs loudly outside.

TO: Shut up! It's going to be difficult to get him to sleep.

TRUNG: Who is it? His laughter is almost inhuman.

TO: He's a debt collector, and he is not afraid of using violence to get money out of people. All right! I don't care whether you laugh or not now! But when the cadre comes, I don't want to hear you laughing like this. If you do, don't blame me for the consequences!

TRAN CONG, SONG ANH *and* THIET *enter the market, smiling.*

TRAN CONG: I am here.

TO: Oh, what a surprise! Mr Cong! And your lovely daughter! When did you arrive? I'll prepare something to—

TRAN CONG: No, no ceremonies, please. This is my secretary Miss Thiet. Consider me like everyone else. Treat me as if I was an ordinary person.

THIET: A pleasure to meet you.

TO: The pleasure is all mine. All of you come out here. I would like to introduce Mr Tran Cong to you all. A summary of his achievements has been distributed to everyone in the market, so they will know who to vote for in the next People's Committee election. He will manage the construction of the new market. Everybody! Bravo!

TRAN CONG: Good morning, everyone!

TRUNG: [*speaking to himself*] That voice, that voice is so familiar. Could it be him? Could it?

NGA: [*surprised*] Excuse me! Are you Mr Cong?

TRAN CONG: What? What are you saying?

NGA: Were you on the Truong Son Trail during the war? I'm not sure, but are you—?

TRAN CONG: Yes, I was fighting on the Truong Son Trail. Were you?

NGA: No, I must be mistaken.

TO: You know, thousands of soldiers fought at Truong Son. It's quite possible for there to be two people who look like each other. But please, it doesn't do any good to bring back those days. The war is over. This is a time of peace.

NGA: Yes, that's true, the war is over, but—

TRAN CONG: Oh, Mr To. Without our yesterdays we can't have our todays, or tomorrows.

TRUNG: [*to himself*] The voice. It could be him.

TRAN CONG: [*pointing*] Mr To, is this area the market?

TO: Yes, it is.

TRAN CONG: It is too sunny! There should be roofs.

TO: Please, wear my hat.

THIET: It's okay, don't worry too much about that. Roofs feature strongly in the design of the new market.

TRAN CONG: Oh! Who's that? Who's lying there?

TO: Ah! He's a war invalid. He's mentally ill because he was wounded in the head.

TRAN CONG: What a pity! How about his parents?

TO: They're both dead. Now Le is looking after him.

SONG ANH: Le! I've been looking for you for so long.

LE: Song Anh.

TRAN CONG: Le, is it difficult to look after him?

LE: I love Thanh very much.

TRAN CONG: To, you have to look after these people. Oh, Miss Thiet! It's so muddy, we must build up the foundations.

THIET: That's right sir! First the roof, second the ground, third the…

TRAN CONG: The what?

THIET: The… third.

TRAN CONG: The People! We must put the People first!

NGA: Oh, we've become accustomed to the sun on our heads and our feet in the mud.

TO: Yes! As Market Manager I will instruct everyone to wear sandals. And wooden sandals too! What's more I will encourage the hat sellers to sell their hats at discount prices! Buy one get one free!

TRAN CONG: Fine! But tell me about the layout of the market?

TO: The people who sell pigs' offal and duck's blood pudding are in the tent where you can hear the music coming from. Their products are renowned in this area, sir!

TRAN CONG: Yes, they have a very good reputation.

THIET: Yes, we must give priority to national specialities. These are good, traditional products of great economic value.

TRAN CONG: They certainly are! And you know, this year is the Year of Tourism. We must have something for the foreigners to see, too.

TO: Yes, sir! This is Mr Trung, who sells traditional duong ho pictures. He has the power of telepathy. Actually, it's more like fortune telling. He can tell people's fortunes simply by listening to their voices, and it's always very accurate… He also gives wonderful massages.

SONG ANH: Is it true that you have the gift of telepathy?

THIET: Fortune telling is not acceptable. We should focus our attention on his gift of massaging.

A dog can be heard barking loudly outside.

TRAN CONG: Dogs! I'm very afraid of dogs! Don't let dogs come into the market! Too many people have died this year as a result of being bitten by rabid dogs.

TRUNG: No, it isn't a dog, it sounds like Tom's voice.

TOM enters, creeping on all fours and barking like a dog.

NGA: Tom!

TOM: Mum! Here's some money!

NGA: Oh, Heavens! Money! How did you get so much money? Tom!

TOM: Today I sold five times more newspapers than I did yesterday.

LE: Is there something sensational in the papers today?

TOM: No! Not at all. It's simple, yesterday I used words, today I tried barking, and it turns out that barking is better.

TRUNG: Why's that?

TOM: It's quite simple! Hearing me barking, people gather round to watch. In between barking I cry out 'Newspapers' and everyone buys a paper from me. It's just like the circus or one of those travelling medicine shows.

TO: Well done! Barking is dogs' business. Selling is the people's business. [*Tapping his glasses*] Glasses are for the intellectual business. You mix them all very well!

TRAN CONG: Is it difficult to bark like that? Where did you learn to do that?

TOM: I learn here. I've learnt in this market. The Market of Lives! It's very easy. Shall I show you?

NGA: Tom, I'd rather be hungry and poor and see you standing on two feet than to witness you doing such—

TOM: If my father was at home I wouldn't have to be a dog. If he wasn't a war hero I wouldn't be so miserable.

NGA: Tom! My son. Your father will come back soon.

TRAN CONG: Excuse me, where is your husband? Why hasn't he returned?

NGA: He's far, very far away.

SONG ANH: Father, is there anything you can do to help her?

TRAN CONG: Wherever he is I can help you and your son find him.

NGA: Thank you. But I know you can't help. He's very far away. [*Crying, and turning away*] He only lives in my memories.

TRAN CONG: I don't understand.

TRUNG: That's his voice! That's his voice!

TO: Mr Trung! Whose voice?

TRUNG: Tran Cong's, the cadre's voice.

TRAN CONG: Why does my voice interest you so much? Do you want to tell my fortune?

TRUNG: I dare not tell yours.

SONG ANH: Please tell my father's fortune. He's very easy going. He once—

TRUNG: —deceived his wife and children, had a son out of wedlock and killed somebody.

TO: Oh! How dare you say such a thing. You have no proof! On what do you base your accusations?

TRUNG: On my feelings.

TO: Mr Trung! Mr Tran Cong is the cadre of the city. You must respect his position.

SONG ANH: Dad! Why are you so quiet? I'll cry if you don't say something! Dad!

TRAN CONG: Blind man! You'll be held responsible for what you've said.

THANH: The truth belongs to those who are not selfish. I would sing about my friends who live for all others.

> [*Singing*] My country in streamlined shape
> Hearing the tender voice of her motherland
> In her struggles against the invaders
> The sons who will never come home
> Their mothers cry quietly…

> THANH *sings in the chaotic atmosphere of the market. The lights go out.*

SCENE TWO

Tran Cong's house. Late afternoon. A large and simple room. SONG ANH *is engrossed in looking for something amongst some documents.* MRS PHUONG, *her mother, enters, silently as a shadow.*

PHUONG: Oh! Song Anh! What are you looking for?

SONG ANH: Mum! You don't know, do you?

PHUONG: [*nervously*] What's the matter?

SONG ANH: People have been gossipping about Dad.

PHUONG: Yes. But it is gossip. Anyone can be the subject of people's talk, my dear.

SONG ANH: But this is different. There is a blind man saying that Dad deceived you, Mum, and has a secret son and… has killed someone.

PHUONG: What?! Where did they say that?

SONG ANH: In the market! The market Dad is directing people to rebuild.

PHUONG: Deceiving you and I, and having a secret son and killing a person! Oh, Anh, no, it's not true! Don't believe it! Who would dare to say such a thing about your father? I'll never believe it. Your father is a good man, a very good man.

SONG ANH: When Dad heard the blind man say those things, he didn't reply. And you know, he's been strange lately. Some nights I wake up and hear him saying horrible things in his sleep, 'crows' and 'blood'. Mum, why don't you ask him what's wrong?

PHUONG: I've already asked him. He says maybe it is because in the day-time he's so busy and tired, at night he has bad dreams.

SONG ANH: Dreams often reflect what has happened during the day. But dreams always come from inside the mind.

PHUONG: Don't be suspicious of him, Song Anh! Life is very complicated. Now, it's quite common for someone to cook up a nasty story about someone else. Especially since your father will be nominated as Vice Chairman of the City People's Committee. You should support your father!

SONG ANH: He's a very courageous man, who once shot down a US war plane and was awarded a medal. I know that.

PHUONG: He's coming, Song Anh. Don't talk about this again.

TRAN CONG *enters*.

TRAN CONG: Good afternoon!

SONG ANH: Hi, Father!

SONG ANH *exits*.

TRAN CONG: What's going on? Why does Song Anh look so edgy?

PHUONG: It's that horrible story they have been telling down in the markets.

TRAN CONG: Oh, is that so? Don't pay any attention to it! It's just market gossip. It's not important. Please, sit down here with me.

PHUONG: It is important because Song Anh has got me worrying now.

TRAN CONG: Oh, just sit down! There's no point in thinking about it.

PHUONG: It's difficult to believe men. You spend so much time travelling, and I know it must be difficult to avoid having affairs with other women.

TRAN CONG: That's not true at all!

PHUONG: Then why would they invent such a story like that, just to discredit you? I must hear this story first hand.

PHUONG *leaves*.

TRAN CONG: Darling! Don't go! Don't. That fortune teller must be arrested for the good of the city. The social and psychological implications of—

SONG ANH *enters and interrupts* TRAN CONG*'s speech.*

SONG ANH: Dad! Who are you talking to?

TRAN CONG: Oh, no one dear. It's a topic of a lecture that I'm giving at the Senior Citizens' Conference. What is all that sugar and milk for?

SONG ANH: People know you're tired, so they have brought some things for you.

TRAN CONG: I've told you not to accept gifts like this. Why did you accept them? Now you have to give them all back.

SONG ANH: I had no choice but to accept them. They insist on putting them here, saying it's a sign of their affection for you.

TRAN CONG: Affection? My dear, there is no such thing as affection.

The sound of Beethoven's Fifth Symphony.

[*Nervously*] Song Anh, what horrible music that is. Turn the radio off, will you please?

SONG ANH: What's the matter, Dad? That's one of Beethoven's most famous symphonies. The theme of the piece is 'Destiny'. It's been so many years since we have been able to listen to Beethoven on the radio.

TRAN CONG: Destiny, destiny! Song Anh, turn it off!

SONG ANH: Mum, can you turn the music down please?

TRAN CONG: It's stuffy in here! Open the windows please.

SONG ANH *opens the windows.*

SONG ANH: Dad! Are you feeling any better?

TRAN CONG: What's that noise?

SONG ANH: Electricians. They're installing lights and banners to celebrate the elections.

TRAN CONG: There's no need for so much light. Oh! Song Anh, I can hear someone crying.

SONG ANH: There's a funeral at one of the houses at the end of the street. A very young soldier died. It's sad to see all those white flowers.

TRAN CONG: [*startled*] Another soldier! Dead! Oh, my dear, what's that bright red on the wall?

SONG ANH: It's sunlight. The sun is bright, red as the eye of fire.

TRAN CONG: Oh, the eye of fire! Close the windows please!

SONG ANH: I'm afraid you'll find it stuffy again.

TRAN CONG: No, I'd rather be hot than see the eye of fire. Oh, Anh, I wish we hadn't gone to the market that day.

SONG ANH: Why?

TRAN CONG: So I wouldn't have heard those things.

SONG ANH: But they can't be true, Dad!

TRAN CONG: No, they're not true. But it makes your mother suspect me, anyway.

SONG ANH: Dad, don't worry so much. I think Mum will believe you. I do.

TU DU *enters, carrying sausages.*

TU DU: Good afternoon!

TRAN CONG: Oh, Du! Come in!

SONG ANH: Why are you carrying sausages, Tu Du?

TU DU: I know you're tired, so I've brought a gift—a couple of kilos of sausages for you.

TRAN CONG: You're too kind. Aren't writers normally a bit stingy? Don't writers never give anything away, even to their future fathers-in-law?

TU DU: Hi hi! Here's my real sign of affection! I've begun writing.

TRAN CONG: Oh, thank you very much! You have to work hard, you know. Sausages are only sausages, fathers-in-law are only fathers-in-law, but literature is for an eternity.

SONG ANH: Is my job as a teacher an eternal job, Dad?

TRAN CONG: Teaching is one of the most noble professions.

TU DU: The Van Nghe Literary Newspaper is planning a special issue on the topic of war.

SONG ANH: Are you going to contribute anything to it?

TU DU: Yes, I am. I want to relate the experiences of my future father-in-law, when he was a soldier on the Truong Son Trail in the great anti-US resistance. You were wounded, Mr Cong, and shot down a US aeroplane. I think it will be great to write about you.

SONG ANH: Oh! You're writing about Dad. You'd better make it good.

TRAN CONG: It's a difficult thing to do. There are some things that we can never understand while we're at war. Only when it's over can we reflect on how terrible it was.

TU DU: I understand! Is it like the foot soldiers whose feet polished the stone on the Trail, who walked all night with torches?

TRAN CONG: Perhaps.

TU DU: Yes, it is the miracle which gave victory to our nation!

TRAN CONG: By the way, do you think the dead can live again?

TU DU: No, I don't think so. But why do you ask me such a strange thing?

TRAN CONG: But do you think a dead man's soul can return and inhabit another person?

TU DU: Oh! Perhaps. It depends on the advances of technology, I suppose. Are you preparing a speech about reincarnation?

TRAN CONG: No… dead people… No, it's the subject for a lecture I'm giving at a seminar on the development of bird-feeding in the city.

SONG ANH: Dad! Dad, what's the matter with you? What have birds got to do with dead people?

TRAN CONG: Oh! What a silly mistake! I've just remembered, it's the topic the board of the Van Dien Cemetery asked me to lecture on.

TU DU: You're very busy indeed.

TRAN CONG: Yes, I'm very busy. There still remain many problems that we have to deal with in our society. You should write about that, about today, don't bring back the war. It's pointless. You weren't in the war, you never fought in the war, so you'll never understand it properly. Don't write about it. [*Pause.*] Can I ask you something else, now? It's about murder. When you see someone else about to die, and you don't help them, is that murder?

TU DU: It depends on the situation.

TRAN CONG: Du, do you think someone with the powers of telepathy can read people's minds and know their secrets?

TU DU: I really don't know about that kind of thing.

TRAN CONG: Yes! But no! Don't repeat this conversation to anyone. This time I will launch a campaign against superstition.

SONG ANH: Dad, you've been behaving so strangely lately. You've been worried and nervous. Why are you paying so much attention to bird raising, cemeteries, Senior Citizens and campaigns against superstition? Your mind used to be on higher things. You used to put a lot of time into congratulating people on their war efforts. Think of all the flags and certificates you gave out!

TRAN CONG: Well, of course I belong to the people. I am their slave. I would do anything for them.

TU DU: I will write about you as a shining example of a devoted cadre.

TRAN CONG: No! Don't write about me! Please!

> TRAN CONG *exits with his head in his hands.*

SONG ANH: You must write something positive about Dad!

TU DU: Believe me, I will immortalise your father's acts of bravery in words.

> *As* SONG ANH *and* TU DU *kiss,* LE *and* THANH *enter.* THANH, *with a guitar, is singing.*

THANH: [*singing*] 'There's a couple kissing each other by the window. Bird's don't fly! Be quiet so they can kiss each other!'

TU DU: Oh, Le! When did you come in? [*Turning to* THANH] It's a pleasure to meet you. I'm Tu Du.

LE: Don't go near him! He's got brain damage! We've just come from the hospital.

TU DU: There's a strange fire in his eyes!

THANH: [*tapping* LE *on the cheek*] Brain damage? What damage do you mean, brain damage? I'm just singing. [*Singing*] 'Let's sing about a fire, with an eager heart of love. Let's sing about love with a flame in your heart…'

SONG ANH: Oh, Le! I'm afraid when he gets like this. What should we do?

TU DU: Don't worry! I'll do something about it.

THANH: Stand up straight. Hey! Artist Thanh greets Great Artist Tu Du.

TU DU: Good afternoon, Mr Thanh.

THANH: [*singing*] 'I can never forget the soldier I met.' I have a new shirt, here! [*Singing*] 'It is the shirt I've been wearing to remember the day—'

TU DU: [*tapping* THANH *on the shoulder*] Beautiful shirt. Come with me and I'll buy you a new pair of trousers.

> THANH *begins singing. They both exit.* LE *is crying.*

SONG ANH: Le, don't cry!

LE: Today people in the market gave me some money to buy a new shirt for him. I was coming to visit you. I have some flowers for you.

SONG ANH: How beautiful! Do you remember when we were still studying at school? Du took us all the way to Ngoc Ha to buy flowers like these.

LE: They're blooming right now in Ngoc Ha, Song Anh.

SONG ANH: Really?

LE: I often take flowers to the market to sell. This is the most beautiful bouquet. I saved it especially for you.

SONG ANH: How happy we were when we were at school. And now…
It's such a pity that Thanh is ill. Oh, Le! I'd like to give you this
bracelet. My father bought it overseas.

LE: It's beautiful. But you should keep it, it suits your hand. It's not
right for me to have it, a cleaner in the market.

SONG ANH: Well, I have this pair of earrings. Would you like them? I'll
give them to you. They were made in Australia.

LE: They're lovely, too. But please keep them. I can't wear them.

SONG ANH: Why not?

LE: When Thanh has a fit he'll snatch at them because they look strange
to him.

SONG ANH: Really? How is your life now?

LE: Filled with tears. Thanh sings all the time, all songs on the radio.
I've made some progress with him but he's not, even for a minute,
aware of what he's doing.

SONG ANH: I understand. Le, why don't you find someone else?

LE: So many people have asked me that. Even his father! When he was
on his deathbed he started crying and he said, 'Le, Le, you marry
someone else. Don't waste your life with Thanh. Let him be. It makes
me unhappy to see you so miserable.'

There is a long silence.

SONG ANH: If that's what he said, why don't you respect his wishes?

LE: I can't leave Thanh, because if I leave him who will look after him?
I still remember the first time I saw him singing in the market. He
looked so vulnerable. How he dreamed of the future, of becoming a
musician. Tu Du is right, there is a flame in his eyes I believe that
the flame will burn more brightly in the future.

A very long silence.

SONG ANH: You can't live in the past. You have no prospects for the
future. Le! Do you understand what I'm saying? You will get older
and your beauty will fade away. Le! Please understand me! You're
still so beautiful.

LE: Am I beautiful?

SONG ANH: Yes, very beautiful. You have to think about yourself. You
must learn to be practical.

LE: Practical! Anh, tell me, what does 'practical' mean?

SONG ANH: Don't you understand? It means that you can't have babies
with mental problems, who are a burden to you and to society.
LE: What? Oh! Babies who… Oh, no, no!

She begins to cry. Outside, THANH *can be heard singing.*

THANH: [*singing*] 'Oh, my country…'
LE: Oh, Thanh, he's singing again. Oh, Thanh!

LE *rushes out of the house.* SONG ANH *follows.* TOM *can be heard
barking outside.* THANH *continues to sing.*

TRAN CONG: [*offstage*] No! No! I didn't do it, it wasn't me. Don't laugh
like that! No, forgive me, please, no, no! Go away!

SONG ANH *quietly goes to the bedroom door. She puts her head in
her hands.* THIET *enters and goes into the bedroom.*

THIET: Mr Cong! I have received a note from the office to come to meet
you after work!
TRAN CONG: Did anyone see you come?
THIET: I don't think so!
TRAN CONG: Good! There is something important I need you to do!
THIET: As your personal secretary, I am always ready to do all you order!
TRAN CONG: Good. Go down to the market and find the blind man. Do
you remember him?
THIET: Yes! I do. That man who said such dreadful things about you!
TRAN CONG: You must find out for me who he is and where he is from.
THIET: I'll find him tomorrow morning first thing.
TRAN CONG: No! You have to go tonight.
THIET: Tonight?
TRAN CONG: Yes! Tonight!
THIET: Why?
TRAN CONG: Don't question me, girl! That is your duty!
THIET: But what can I do with a blind man in the middle of the night?
TRAN CONG: Do whatever he wants! Do whatever men want to do in the
night. I need to know who he is! [*Whispering*] Understand? I will
give you money right now if you agree!
THIET: I've never stooped that low! People will call me a… a prostitute!
TRAN CONG: Who'll know? Anyway, it is your duty. Good Communists
have to know and learn how to sacrifice themselves for the wonderful
future of the country and its people. I will recognise you as a silent
hero if you do as I ask.

THIET: If not…?

TRAN CONG: If not…! I don't know! There is a mountain of people applying for your job! It will be very quick! Everything means nothing in the darkness!

THIET: I could do what you're asking with you, but please don't ask me to do it with that blind man. He looks like an animal. He is dangerous!

TRAN CONG: You want to have sex with the married leader of the government. You are such a naughty secretary!

THIET: What is the difference between having sex with you and with him?

TRAN CONG: Don't talk back. The first is a revolutionary duty and the second is immoral sexual corruption! Understand?

THIET: Yes. I understand.

TRAN CONG: [*giving* THIET *money*] Watch your mouth! Go quickly before the moon rises.

Blackout.

SCENE THREE

The market. It is raining heavily and THANH *is singing in the rain.* MRS PHUONG *is holding an umbrella. Thunder is rumbling in the distance.*

PHUONG: Where is everybody? Who can tell me why people say these things? Why my husband and no one else? Has he really been deceiving me? Does he really have a son with someone else? Did he murder someone? No! No! He's a virtuous and even-tempered man. He's never raised a hand against his child. Even my friends are envious of our relationship. But now what will they think? Who will offer me a word of comfort in this dark market? I can feel everyone laughing at me. Well, I'd like to ask all you wives, if you've ever loved your husband what do you do when his name is blackened? But still, there's no smoke without a fire… Oh, Cong! Is it true? No, no! Then why? Maybe they don't like you, and that is why they have made up these stories. Please! Rain! Wind, keep howling! Thunder! Rumble on! Everybody listen! My husband is a good man. No one knows this better than I do!

PHUONG *leaves. Later that night, the rain has stopped. It is quiet. The moon is shining brightly.* MR TRUNG *is sitting in the middle of the market.* TOM *is spoon-feeding him rice soup.*

TOM: Mr Trung, please try to eat some more to help you sweat it out. You're getting feverish again.

TRUNG: Oh, leave me alone. It's dark. Your mother will be waiting up for you. Go home!

TOM: I'm not going to leave till you finish this soup. Oh, Mr Trung, why don't you come to my house? It's cold tonight, and you have a fever.

TRUNG: No, no, I can't.

TOM: Well, if you won't come with me, I'm going to sleep here with you. I can't leave you here alone at night.

TRUNG: Don't worry about me, Tom. Is the moon very bright tonight?

TOM: Yes, it is.

TRUNG: The clouds are passing across the moon, aren't they?

TOM: Oh, yes! A black cloud looks like it is going to swallow the moon. How did you know?

TRUNG: Because I can hear the crows crying. Long ago in Truong Son, there were nights when the moon shone brightly. But whenever the moon was covered I would hear the crows crying.

TOM: Really?

TRUNG: Yes, really! It must be very dark! You should leave now. Tomorrow you have to sell newspapers.

TOM: Tomorrow I'll sell more pictures for you.

TRUNG: Yes, thanks!

TOM: Let me make your bed for you before I leave. Hey, where's your mosquito net?

TRUNG: It's been stolen.

TOM: Damn thief! I'll bring mine. Just wait a minute.

TOM *runs out. A crow's cry can be heard.*

TRUNG: Oh! Tom! That's the crow crying. It's a bad omen. I will pray for you.

THIET *enters.*

I hear a frightened breath mixing with the crow crying in the market. Who is there? What makes you breathe like that? Can I help you?

THIET: [*frightened*] Please tell me who you are.

TRUNG: A voice of a young girl. Why are you in the market at this time of night? Everybody has gone home. Why are you still here?

THIET: I've come to ask you who you are? Please tell me who you are?

TRUNG: Why do you want to know about me?

THIET: Please tell me. If not…

TRUNG: If not…?

THIET: I will lose my job.

TRUNG: You will lose your job!

THIET: [*scared to go to* TRUNG] Yes, I will.

   A long pause.

TRUNG: Come here!

THIET: [*sitting down and intending to take her shirt off*] You can do whatever you want with me! I'm ready!

TRUNG: I hear the sound of single buttons opening when you take your shirt off. You must be a very beautiful young girl because the night is suddenly quiet, the wind has stopped blowing, the crow has stopped crying. Tell me. Do you have someone special who you love in your heart?

THIET: Yes, I do. And you?

TRUNG: Yes, from a long time ago.

THIET: Where is she now?

TRUNG: She is somewhere among the forests of people. In the wind, under the moonlight, in every beat of my heart.

THIET: You must love her very much!

TRUNG: Tell me. What do you want with me, the old blind man of the market? Your lover will be very sad if he knew about this!

THIET: Please, keep this secret! This business is between you and me. My boss wants to know about you! He asked me to do this. I didn't want to but you said something that disturbed him.

TRUNG: Your boss? Said something that disturbed him…? Tran Cong!

THIET: Yes! He is a war hero! He is very powerful! I have money here. I have my body. You can have whatever you want, just tell me who you are!

TRUNG: I am a blind man who sells traditional pictures in the market. You can tell him that I am just a blind man who sells traditional pictures in the market.

THIET: [*touching* TRUNG] He wants to know more than that!

TRUNG: Don't touch me! Every part of my body is dead already, there is only an empty space for the moonlight in my heart. Please go. Go to the man you love and make him feel that love is peace, beauty and happiness, not a game of deception and sorrow.

THIET: Listen to you. I don't understand but I feel there is something very special in your words. Something that makes people still want to live and care for each other…

> THIET *exits.*

TRAN CONG: [*walking in on tiptoe*] Mr Trung! Mr Trung!

TRUNG: Who's that? Who's calling my name in the night?

TRAN CONG: It's me! Can you help me?

TRUNG: What? [*Shouting loudly*] Don't come round pretending to be a friend and steal my money! I only have one mosquito net, and somebody has already stolen it! Go away! I won't be fooled again!

> MRS NGA *enters with a mosquito net in her hands. When she sees* TRAN CONG *she hides in the shadows.*

TRAN CONG: Shhh, shhh, don't shout. It's me! I'm not here to rob you, I've come to ask you something.

TRUNG: That voice, that voice again.

TRAN CONG: Yes, it's me, it's Tran Cong. You have a sharp sense of hearing and a very good memory.

TRUNG: Why did you come here at night?

TRAN CONG: I've come to see you. I'm very busy in the day-time.

TRUNG: I told you about yourself, didn't I?

TRAN CONG: Yes, you did! When I came here to survey the markets you said I was deceiving my wife and daughter, that I have a secret child and that I murdered someone. I've been obsessed with it ever since. Now there's only you and I. Tell me, why did you say those things?

TRUNG: You were very sure of yourself to come back then. Now why are you trembling?

> *A crow cries.*

TRAN CONG: Oh, I'm cold. The fog is so cold. Mr Trung, what's that sound?

TRUNG: That is a crow crying.

TRAN CONG: Why does that sound make me tremble? Answer my question for my own peace of mind! Tell me!

TRUNG: Is there a scar on the left side of your chest?

TRAN CONG: Yes, there is. I've had it since the war.

TRUNG: Another soldier carried you on his back, didn't he, through many kilometres of jungle to a military hospital?

TRAN CONG: Yes, that's right! But—

TRUNG: Come here! Come near me! Take off your shirt and kneel down.

TRAN CONG: [*backing off*] Why do I have to kneel down?

TRUNG: Kneel down! I want to see what your scar is like now.

TRAN CONG: Here! Here's my chest.

TRUNG: [*touching* TRAN CONG'*s chest*] Here it is! Here it is. I knew it, it's your voice. It's your chest. And inside your body flows the blood of an evil man. It's you, Tran Khanh.

TRAN CONG: How do you know my real name?

TRUNG: The scar! The scar is still here. But with a different name. Have you forgotten already? Remember Co Tien Hill Pass?

TRAN CONG: Such a beautiful place!

TRUNG: So much blood and so many tears were shed.

TRAN CONG: We were surrounded by spies, US war planes had destroyed the strategic road.

TRUNG: This road is so important! I'm the Leader of our Battalion

TRAN CONG: I take control of the machine gun. My name is Tran Khanh.

TRUNG: I ordered you to shoot the enemy down with so much ammunition—

TRAN CONG: —that I could aim with my eyes closed. I wasn't afraid of running out of bullets.

TRUNG: It was twilight. Khanh! Shoot! What are you waiting for? Shoot now!

TRAN CONG: Trung, hide! F-111s are coming!

> TRUNG *pushes* TRAN CONG *out of the way and takes control of the machine gun.*

TRUNG: Come on, Americans, I'll blast you out of the sky!

TRAN CONG: [*hiding*] Trung, it's firing rockets at us!

TRUNG: I think I've hit it! I'll— [*Screaming and falling to the ground*] Aaaah! Khanh! It's dark! My eyes, I can't see! Help me, help! Where's the sun?!

TRAN CONG: Trung, what's happened to your eyes? Did the rockets—?

TRUNG: I'm blind! Khanh! Help me, please!

TRAN CONG: [*pretending*] I'm… I'm hurt too!

TRUNG: Khanh! You can see, help me, Khanh!

TRAN CONG: [*to himself*] Khanh! Think of yourself. This is your big chance! On the right is a sheer drop, on your left is the forest. Left or right, right or left? Trung! Make your way to the right… to safety, to the right.

TRUNG: [*sliding over the edge of the cliff and screaming*] Aaaah! Khanh, help me! Help me, I can't feel anything under my feet. Am I going to fall? Help me, I can't hold on much longer.

TRAN CONG: Trung! You're blind! What's the point of living if you're blind?

TRUNG: Khanh, help me, have pity on me! I'm my mother's only son!

TRAN CONG: Trung! Forgive me! You're blind, your life is worthless! Better to die now!

He walks away from TRUNG.

TRUNG: [*screaming*] You've betrayed me!

He collapses.

TRAN CONG: I betrayed a friend. But from now on I won't be called Tran Khanh anymore. I'll change my name to Tran Cong, and take credit for shooting down that plane. I'll be a hero.

NGA: [*from outside*] Everybody, everybody gather round! This is Mr Khanh. A hero! He shot down an F-111! He saved the military hospital, he saved the lives of hundreds of injured soldiers. Mr Khanh! I love you so much!

TRAN CONG: Please, from now on my name is Cong.

NGA: Cong, I love that name. It means great achievement.

TRAN CONG: You're my young bamboo shoot of the Truong Son Trail.

NGA *exits.*

TRUNG: So, you still remember?

TRAN CONG: No! It's not true. You're lying.

TRUNG: I didn't tell your fortune, I just told the truth.

TRAN CONG: But it wasn't me! You've got it all wrong!

TRUNG: You can change your name and your appearance, but you can't change your conscience. Wake up to yourself! Face the reality of what you've done.

TRAN CONG: How can a blind man in the market know this? Or has Trung's soul inhabited this old man? Then why does he look so much like Trung? Oh, Budda, it really is him, it's Trung. Oh, Trung, forgive me! I've been praying for you all these years. I went to Truong Son Trail to build a shrine for you by the abyss. I looked after your mother until she died. I often tell Phuong about you. Now we have a happy family and a daughter. Take pity on me! Don't hate me!

TRUNG: Phuong? A happy family? Yes, it's me, Hoang Van Trung.

TRAN CONG: But no, it can't be. How could you survive that fall? I saw your body hitting the ground.

TRUNG: A Buddist monk rescued me and sheltered me under the roof of the temple.

TRAN CONG: And now you're standing here in front of me.

TRUNG: Yes!

TRAN CONG: You're getting very old. And the scars have made your face look so wrinkled.

TRUNG: I can't see what your face looks like. But I heard you panting like an animal when I unmasked you. And I can smell you. You smell like a scared man. And that's enough for me to know what you look like now.

TRAN CONG: Trung! I beg you! Don't curse me! I've changed my ways. I've done so much to atone for my mistakes. I've devoted myself to serving the people. I've helped to make this nation great once more. That's why I'm here to rebuild this market.

TRUNG: What will you name the market?

TRAN CONG: What? Hasn't it already got a name?

TRUNG: Ah, yes! Market of Lives—that's its name. But you must remember that its foundations should be built on honesty, purity and kindness, not lies and deception.

TRAN CONG: I know, I know. People believe in me. People are relying on me to rebuild this market.

TRUNG: You don't deserve their trust. You should confess your crimes.

> *The crow's cry can be heard.*

TRAN CONG: It's that crow again. How can I make it stop?

TRUNG: Only the arrival of daylight will stop the crow from calling.

TRAN CONG: No, please don't force me to confess. My reputation will be destroyed. Everything I've done will come to nothing.

TRUNG: You haven't changed. You once tried to kill your friend to advance your position. Now you're betraying people's trust in you by building a market to get their support, so once again you can improve your standing in the community. You're always thinking of yourself, never of others.

TRAN CONG: Let me be your servant. I'll do anything you want. I'll give you a job, a house… How about a trip overseas?

TRUNG: And a young girl… Such a bad man, his mind never changes.

TRAN CONG: Please, please don't force me to confess.

TRUNG: It's too easy to keep on deceiving people. You must tell the truth!

TRAN CONG: Oh, Trung! Why? Why are you threatening me? Why do you want me to change everything for you? What for? Why?

TRUNG: For everyone else's sake. For the future of this market, you must confess!

TRAN CONG: [*picking up a stone*] I will…

TRUNG: You can never kill me again. Years ago you couldn't kill me in the quiet of the jungle. Now you cannot kill me in the market.

TRAN CONG: I will make my confession in front of everyone. I swear. But you, you must never tell them who you are. Just keep on being the blind man who sells pictures in the market, forever.

TRUNG: Why? Why should I do that?

TRAN CONG: Because I don't want Phuong, my wife, to hate me. We've been happily married for years. Don't dig up my terrible past in front of her! It will only upset her. You belong to the past as far as she is concerned.

TRUNG: Phuong! Your wife! Yes! Yes! Never! Yes! Get out!

> TRAN CONG *goes and* MRS NGA *rushes in.*

NGA: Trung! I was bringing a mosquito net for you and I heard what was going on! It's me! I was Truong Son Trail's young bamboo shoot! How come we didn't recognise each other? Why didn't you recognise me?

TRUNG: Truong Son Trail's young bamboo shoot. Nga! Is that Nga?

NGA: Why didn't we recognise each other?

TRUNG: Pain has changed us. But why are you living here, in this market?

NGA: I've been looking for someone, just like you. And imagine, it's the same person we're looking for!

TRUNG: Tran Cong?

NGA: Yes! I recognised him when he came to the market that first time. I was going to rush up to him and hug him. I was going to say: 'Tom, this is your father. Come and see your father.'

TRUNG: Why didn't you? It would've made Tom happy? Is Tom really his son?

NGA: Yes, just after the fighting I concealed the truth because he was about to be awarded a medal for being a hero. And a hero can never make a mistake, even if it's only a mistake caused by love.

TRUNG: Is that so?

NGA: Even when I met him in the market I couldn't stop thinking: 'He's a hero.' And no hero can have a son pretending to be a dog so he can sell his newspapers, and a poor wife who has to sell herbs in the market.

TRUNG: Nga! In my mind, you're just like you used to be on Truong Son.

NGA: No, this time I won't hide the truth, I'll confront him. I'll let everyone know who he is and what he's done.

TRUNG: No, Nga, don't do that! For Phuong's sake! Don't tell the truth! You'll spoil everything for her. She has a happy family, as good a life as any woman could hope for. She believes in her husband. She'll be so unhappy if she knows the truth. Let her think she's happy. Please, Nga, don't denounce him.

NGA: Trung! All right I won't do it. I won't denounce him… for you!

TRUNG: We grow up when we learn how to forgive. The truth of the moon will shine through the darkness.

NGA and TRUNG *stand under the bright moonlight. Blackout.*

SCENE FOUR

Morning in Tran Cong's house. PHUONG *is worried. She is waiting for someone to phone.* TU DU *is sitting by the table, writing.*

TU DU: [*writing*] 'The soldiers set forth along the Truong Son Trail to drive out the enemy and liberate the country.' Yes! That sounds great!

PHUONG: Du! Have some lunch! You've been writing since this morning, you must be hungry.

TU DU: Yes, but don't worry about it. I've got something interesting here. Oh! The image I have of your husband is very clear in my mind. Let me read this passage to you!

PHUONG: Yes, read it please!

TU DU: [*reading*] 'There's one man from Ha Noi, destined to be a hero, marching with the troops along the Truong Son Trail…'

PHUONG: Oh, yes, that's it.

TU DU: [*reading*] 'His great name is Cong and his family name is Tran. He's thinking of the girl he loves. A girl with long hair and eyes as sparkling and clear as the water in Truc Back Lake…'

PHUONG: It's a good start. But you shouldn't reveal his name first off. And secondly, the eyes should be described as 'sparkling and as clear as the water in Autumn'.

TU DU: [*making a note*] Ah yes, good point, I'll correct that.

PHUONG: Please, continue!

TU DU: [*reading*] 'In extremely difficult conditions, oblivious to pain and hardship, our soldier annihilates the enemy's planes…'

PHUONG: Don't you think that's a little strong?

TU DU: Oh, yes, but leave it like that. The editorial board will tone it down.

PHUONG: Have you written about what was happening at home?

TU DU: Yes, I've written a section called 'Letter from the Front Line Covered with Tears'.

PHUONG: And, you know, at that you point you should be talking about the war planes.

TU DU: Yes, yes. [*Writing it down*] 'One after another the bombers…'

PHUONG: But what was it like on the ground when the planes were coming? I wasn't there.

TU DU: Neither was I. Ah! Yes, now I remember, I read somewhere that someone described it as 'a rain of bombs, falling'.

PHUONG: Well yes, of course there were a lot of bombs falling, but you need a strong image to convey what it was like on the ground.

TU DU: Ah, mangoes, what about bombs falling like mangoes? Oh, I like that: [*writing*] 'bombs raining like mangoes falling'.

PHUONG: And the soldier was wounded on his left breast.

TU DU: [*taking notes*] 'His left breast…'

PHUONG: He still bears the scar.

TU DU: [*writing*] 'He still bears the scar…'

PHUONG: Why are you writing that?

TU DU: Oh!

PHUONG: And now what are you going to write?

TU DU: It's only the first draft. Part one of the memoirs. The next scene is firecrackers, flowers, decorative lighting, cheering, adulation. The elections. I've got it all in my mind. 'His greatest triumph.' It'll be a fantastic scene.

PHUONG: As it should be. The elections are close at hand. These memoirs will put a stop to those nasty rumours.

TU DU: Don't worry. As soon as Mr Cong gives his permission, we can publish the memoirs. Oh! I've got to go. There's a professor giving a lecture today on Honesty in Literature.

PHUONG: Oh, all right, well hurry up, off you go, otherwise you'll be late.

TU DU: 'Bye!

> TU DU *goes quickly.* TRUNG *appears at the door.*

PHUONG: Who are you?

TRUNG: Excuse me, is this Tran Cong's house?

PHUONG: Yes, it is. Do you want to see him?

TRUNG: I'm the blind man from the market, I sell pictures. Were you looking for me a few days ago?

PHUONG: Oh! You're that man?

TRUNG: Yes, I am.

PHUONG: Please, here's a chair, sit down.

TRUNG: Thank you. What did you want to see me for?

PHUONG: [*getting all fired up*] Why have you been spreading such malicious rumours about my husband?

TRUNG: Malicious rumours?

PHUONG: Yes. My husband is a cadre, much respected in the community. Why have you tried to humiliate him like that?

TRUNG: Humiliate?

PHUONG: Yes. Don't you understand? My husband's good reputation is being questioned because of your stories. You think the sound of someone's voice can tell you everything about them. Well, it can't. Voices can't tell you anything.

TRUNG: Voices can help people to recognise each other.

PHUONG: When I hear you, I hear the voice of someone who wants to make people unhappy.
TRUNG: I don't mean to hurt you. From the sound of your voice I think you must sing beautifully. But only sad songs.
PHUONG: Are you telling me my fortune? Well, yes, it's true, when I was young I used to love singing sad songs. 'Giot Mua Thu'—'Rain in Autumn'.
TRUNG: It's the line, 'a life is a sea of troubles', in that song?
PHUONG: Yes, it is. Go on! Why are you so quiet?
TRUNG: Is it raining? I can hear the sound of raindrops falling into a small glass fish pond, with rock-work in the middle.
PHUONG: [*going to the window*] You have wonderful hearing. It really is raining. And the glass basin is there, but the rock-work is broken. But how did you know there was a glass fish pond in the garden of my house?
TRUNG: I had an image of it in my mind. It just turns out to be true.
PHUONG: It's true. Long ago when I was young… Oh! I nearly forgot, would you like some water? Some coffee? I'll pour some coffee for you.
TRUNG: You make very nice coffee, perhaps you used to make coffee for your parents, very thick with no sugar. Just hearing you speak now I can tell you're thinking about something in the past.
PHUONG: Yes, but they're just memories. From long, long ago. Listening to you I feel like what you've said about my husband might be true… I wonder if it could…
TRUNG: No, you shouldn't think about it.
PHUONG: If it's true, you'll have to tell me why you said those things.
TRUNG: Do you really need to know?
PHUONG: Yes, I do. Because I believe my husband is a good man.
TRUNG: Well, you should believe him. A wife needs to be able to trust her husband.
PHUONG: Then why did you humiliate him? You can tell the truth about rain and coffee, but what you said about my husband is much more important. I don't believe it. Do you hate him?
TRUNG: No, don't think like that, please!
PHUONG: But why?
TRUNG: I… I may have mistaken him for someone else.

PHUONG: Oh! Why are you crying! I'm so sorry.

TRUNG: I have no more tears to cry. It's just, it's just I have an image of you in my mind, crying. Your long dark hair. Your shining eyes, your delicate cheekbones. Long ago! Long ago there was a man who wanted to paint your beauty, like Michelangelo painting Venus. And then the war came. Everything changed. And you pushed those memories down, memories of a youth who loved you, but left to fight for his country… and never returned to marry you.

PHUONG: Heaven and Earth! That's it exactly. How did you know? You seem to have an understanding… How could you know these things about my past? Who are you?

TRUNG: I'm a fortune teller.

PHUONG: But what you've said brings back so many painful memories. It's true, the war took my love from me, and broke my heart.

TRUNG: He wasn't killed by bombs or bullets. He was betrayed…

PHUONG: I didn't betray him. He wanted to paint me but then the war came, and he went to the front… I never thought I'd lose him. I kept leaves in books to count the days he was away. I waited for him! I waited and waited, until Tran Cong appeared in the last days of the war. He had a medal for bravery pinned to his chest, and he told me that my lover had been killed.

TRUNG: And you believed him?

PHUONG: Yes. I was so unhappy, and he made me believe he could replace my lover. I needed to believe in something. And he was a hero, devoted to his country.

TRUNG: So different.

PHUONG: Why do you say that? Do you know them?

TRUNG: No, no, I don't.

PHUONG: Looking at you, your mouth, your nose, I feel like you're him. You're so like him!

TRUNG: No, no! You're mistaken. I'm just a blind man who sells pictures in the market.

PHUONG: It is you! How could I not recognise you? Trung! That explains everything. You're Trung!

>   TRAN CONG *enters.*

TRAN CONG: Oh! What are you doing here? What have you been telling my wife?

TRUNG: I told her that I was mistaken. That I mistook you for someone else.

TRAN CONG: Are you sure it's a mistake?

TRUNG: Yes.

TRAN CONG: Phuong, what did he tell you? You know my life is devoted to you.

PHUONG: Cong! I'm confused, Cong! Don't you think he looks like Trung?

TRAN CONG: Trung? Who's Trung? Ah, yes, maybe. Maybe a little bit like him. Trung's nose was higher, Trung's eyes were nicer. Don't talk of the dead, let him rest in peace.

PHUONG: No! Look at him carefully! It's him. I don't believe he died. I don't.

>   PHUONG *runs out.*

TRAN CONG: What did you tell her?

TRUNG: The past! The past made bitter and sad by your deception.

TRAN CONG: The past, the past! Did she recognise you?

TRUNG: I don't know. How could I know?

TRAN CONG: I thought we had an agreement. Keep quiet. Do you want to destroy my family?

TRUNG: You're afraid of the truth!

TRAN CONG: That's not the point. I want everything to be okay until after the election.

TRUNG: The people will be fooled again. That's the point!

TRAN CONG: You don't understand anything. There are certain things you can't do when you're a politician. Leave my life alone. Don't ruin my career.

TRUNG: I'll keep my word. But you must do this—just before voting begins you must make your confession in front of the People. You can't mislead the children of the market. Future generations must know the truth. I want you to come clean. So does your conscience, Tran Khanh.

TRAN CONG: Never! Hoang Van Trung, I will never confess! You can go and denounce me. But watch out, you might be accused of slander.

TRUNG: I believe in justice.

TRAN CONG: Of course, everyone believes in justice. But what evidence do you have that I'm guilty? Do you have any at all? Only you and I know what happened on the Truong Son Trail. No one will believe you. So be careful, Trung. No one will even believe you're still alive.

TRUNG: What? What? Why is it so quiet? Is there nobody here who believes me?

TRAN CONG: [*smiling*] See? Nobody. No one will believe you, Trung, no one will believe you. [*He laughs.*] Go away, Trung.

> TRUNG *leaves. The sound of a stick on the street can be heard outside.*

You see, no one believes you, Trung, no one believes you.

> *He laughs.* SONG ANH *enters.*

SONG ANH: Who are you talking to, Father?

TRAN CONG: Nobody, don't worry about it.

> MR TO *rushes in from behind the fence.*

TO: Oh, here you are, Mr Cong. It's so tense down in the markets. I can't stand it any longer. I've come to resign as Market Manager.

TRAN CONG: What's going on?

SONG ANH: Good morning, Mr To. What's happened?!

TO: My Buddha, the market is in chaos! Understand?!

> THANH*'s voice can be heard from outside, gradually receding.*

THANH: Mr Cong, the market is falling apart, the market is falling apart. Mr Cong!

TO: Oh, that weirdo! Shut up, get out of here!

SONG ANH: [*calling out*] Thanh!

TRAN CONG: Mr To, what do you mean, 'chaos'?

TO: The gamblers were fighting over some money, and a huge brawl developed.

TRAN CONG: Is everybody all right?

TO: One dead, two injured. They're still slugging it out down there, I think.

TRAN CONG: Keep calm. Sit down.

TO: How can I be calm in this situation? Yesterday a young girl deliberately walked three times around the market without her trousers, for a few thousand dong. The handcart men bet her to do it. When I got there, she walked around again one more time before she put her trousers back on.

SONG ANH: That explains what happened when I was doing teacher training at the primary school yesterday. When I began talking about the National Heroic Women, the children started laughing uncontrollably. It's so important to instil in them proper moral values.

TRAN CONG: Don't blame the children. It's your duty to teach them what's right and what's wrong. But when they grow up, they have to make their own choices.

SONG ANH: Well, is that so?

TO: That's not all. Just the other day a scrap dealer, in love with the girl who sells noodle soup, stole his mother's gold to give to the girl. The mother found out and there was a huge fight right in the middle of the market.

SONG ANH: Really?

TO: And there's more. An old beggar threw a handful of mud into another man's bowl of noodle soup, just because the man didn't give him any money. And then the man forced the poor old beggar to eat it.

TRAN CONG: The new market is not yet built but the old one is in a shambles. How could this have happened? You're supposed to be in charge.

TO: Well, I'm a very busy man. I can't take care of everything. I can't read people's minds. How can I tell if this person or that person is going to do something stupid?

TRAN CONG: Where is your revolutionary will?

TO: For Budda's sake, don't mention revolutionary will at a time like this. You know, my best friend lives near Hang Co Station, but I daren't go to see him because of the thieves and gangsters in that area. All I can do is write him letters.

> TRAN CONG *and* MR TO *both laugh.*

TRAN CONG: Well, you may as well go now.

> TOM *enters as a dog.*

TO: Tom, what are you doing here, what's wrong?

TOM: Mr To! Mr To! Trung is dead!

TO: What?

TOM: The gamblers were fighting and one of them was brandishing a huge knife.

TO: And then what happened?

TOM: Mr Trung threw himself into the fight, trying to stop them. And he's blind so he couldn't see anything.

TO: Oh, Budda!

TOM: I got there too late. There was blood everywhere.

TO: Oh, Mr Trung!

SONG ANH: Father, I'm so frightened!

TRAN CONG: Mr To, you'll prepare a suitable burial for the poor man, won't you?

TO: Yes, I will.

> *All except* TRAN CONG *leave.* THIET *appears behind the fence.*

TRAN CONG: Trung! That's the end. All my troubles will leave with you now. But why did you behave like you did? You were so stupid. Who were you to tell people what to do? Who are you to advise people in this mad life?

> *He laughs a satisfied but bitter laugh. The voice of* THANH *can be heard outside.*

THANH: Ha ha ha, be so foolish. [*Singing*] 'All your friends are still here, your lover's here, too. Then you'll have to leave them all. Oh, time goes by. A man's footprints will fade.'

SCENE FIVE

The market at night. Everything is lying about in disarray. In the centre is a shrine for TRUNG. *It is cold and quiet.* TRAN CONG *sits at the shrine.* PHUONG *quietly enters and hides behind the shrine. A group of people circle around* TRAN CONG, *representing his conscience.*

TRAN CONG: Trung! Why did this happen to you? Why couldn't you live to tell everybody that what you said about me was wrong. The elections are tomorrow. How will people trust me now? Why aren't you still alive? If you were still alive I could make up for what I have done. You came and went, and now people think I'm a criminal. Trung, I'm not guilty. We used to be best friends in the old days. All this is because of the war. Just one mistake has ruined my life… And you know this world is full of mistakes. Trung! You've led a noble life and died out of love for your fellow human beings. I beg your soul to help the new market. The new market will put the past to rest, both the war and our story. Trung, I beg you witness my honesty. Who are you? Past, present or future?

The CHORUS *enters.*

CHORUS 1: You can never bury the past.

CHORUS 2: It always leaves its trace on the present.

CHORUS 3: You can't wipe it away.

ALL CHORUS: Trung has died.

CHORUS 4: But we are still living.

CHORUS 5: And others will live after us.

ALL CHORUS: To die and live mean nothing.

CHORUS 6: Perhaps when a man dies he can leave everything behind, forget about everything, but he can't run away from himself while he's alive.

ALL CHORUS: Life is life.

CHORUS 7: And remember that this life must be built on a foundation of…

ALL CHORUS: … purity, goodwill and a clear conscience.

CHORUS 8: Not deception, dishonesty and selfish pride.

CHORUS 4: Mum, I've earned money from this damned newspaper to help you. Why are you angry at me?

CHORUS 1: Tom, my dear, you can't see this life clearly if you live it like a dog.

CHORUS 5: There is no reason to keep him believing that this muddy drain is a beautiful garden and that this street market is paradise.

CHORUS 8: Dad, I'll have to tell my pupils the truth, so that they'll see they must build a better society.

ALL CHORUS: Life is life.

The circle of people disappears. The dream ends.

TRAN CONG: Where are you? Where? Trung? Is that your people who are speaking?

Dawn. A boy somewhere is crying out 'Newspapers'. TOM *enters.*

TOM: Papers, papers! Here's the latest news! Market to be rebuilt! Election of the People's Committee today. Good morning, Mr Cong. Do you want a newspaper? Why are you here so early? Look, your hair's all wet with dew.

TRAN CONG: Give me a newspaper, boy.

He puts the newspaper at the foot of the shrine.

TOM: Why did you put it there?

TRAN CONG: So that Mr Trung can read it too.

MR TO *enters with* MRS NGA.

TO: As the Market Manager, I order you to take away this shrine.

NGA: I won't let you!

TO: Why not? We all feel sorry about what happened to Mr Trung, but this shrine is taking up valuable space. Get rid of it.

TRAN CONG: What's the problem, Mr To?

TO: Oh, you're here. You can help me deal with this. This situation is intolerable.

SONG ANH *and* TU DU *rush in.*

SONG ANH: Father, where have you been?

TU DU: Good morning, Mr Cong.

TRAN CONG: Good morning. I was here.

TU DU: This will be a wonderful detail for the memoirs.

TO: Oh, Mr Cong, They're coming. It's turning to chaos.

TRAN CONG: Who?

TO: Well, this shrine was set up by Mrs Nga. It occupies the space assigned to Mrs Nga, but also Mrs Thin, who sells boiled shellfish. Mrs Thin wants to get rid of it, while Mrs Nga doesn't. And as a result, the whole market is taking sides. Early this morning, Mrs Thin went to her village to fetch some men. Here they come!

TU DU: Take it down, Mr Cong. He wasn't a hero.

THIET: Cong? I'd like to say how unsightly it is. When the new market is finished, how can you keep this here?

TO: Look, here they come! Do something, Mr Cong!

NGA: I beg you. Show him some respect please. Don't do that. He was blind because of you all and died because of you all. Why do you begrudge him this tiny piece of land?

TOM: No one can touch it.

TRAN CONG: Everybody, we'll erect a memorial here on which we'll write very clearly: 'This is the place of worship of Mr Hoang Van Trung, the hero of the Truong Son Trail'.

NGA: Trung, I'm still afraid that he won't honour his promise.

TRAN CONG: Who are you?

NGA: It's me, I was the young bamboo shoot of the Truong Son Trail.

TRAN CONG: What?

NGA: Remember Co Tien Hill Pass?

TRAN CONG: You!

NGA: Yes, it's me. I recognised you the first day you came to the market. But you didn't recognise me. Cong, this is Tom. Your son. You can't ignore him now. He's part of the future of this market, and he's our child. He was born when we were both young, during the war.

TRAN CONG: Tom?

NGA: Those nights in Truong Son jungle. Don't you remember? Tom, come to your father.

TRAN CONG: My past is haunting me today.

NGA: No, it's your conscience haunting you. Be brave. Just for once in your life. Tom, come here to your father.

Pause of three beats.

SONG ANH: Dad, is this true? Everything the poor blind man said was true?

TRAN CONG: Yes, my dear. It's the truth.

SONG ANH: What am I going to tell my pupils tomorrow? What am I going to make them believe in now?

TRAN CONG: Please forgive me, my dear.

SONG ANH: Dad, how can I believe in you now?

TU DU: The memoirs, I've spent so much time over them. I'm up to page three hundred and twenty-seven!

TRAN CONG: Burn them, Du. It's all lies.

Everyone jumps when suddenly…

PHUONG: Trung. Why didn't you recognise me? Why? I've waited for you for so long. [*To* TRAN CONG] For so many tortured nights I've heard you confess everything in your dreams. [*To* TRUNG] You've made my life so miserable and bitter.

TRAN CONG: Phuong. Please, call down curses upon me, but don't look at me like that.

PHUONG: I believed in you my whole life. I thought I was important to you. I existed only for you. I was wrong.

PHUONG *leaves, dejectedly.* THIET *enters.*

THIET: Mr Cong! You can have your money back. I am resigning, I'm going to find another. I want to help the people rebuild this market.

TU DU: We are living in strange and stormy times. Everybody, let's get together and build the new market! I'll write about this market, and this time I'll write the truth.

TO: Be quiet, be quiet. Do you hear anything? It's funny old Thanh singing. Well, how beautifully he sings today! There, can you hear him?

THANH: [*singing*] My country in streamlined shape
   Hearing the tender voice of our motherland
   In her struggles against the invaders
   The people who will never come home
   Their mothers cry quietly.

THE END

Meat Party

Translated by Lien Yeomans

Translation edited by Rachel Hennessy

*This play is dedicated to the souls
of those who died in all the wars on this earth with the hope that
they will be reborn into a peaceful world.*

* * *

*The characters and events of this play are fictional
and created with the hope that
they will contribute to the elimination of all wars.*

CHARACTERS

MARY, flautist, speaks fluently the local language of the White Sand Desert, daughter of Gabriel Wallis, aged 30

CRONE, a lonely old woman who lives in the White Sand Desert where many bloody battles occurred during the war, aged 78

LAM, retired army officer, one half of his face is badly scarred from burns, war hero, old comrade-in-arms with An, aged 68

GABRIEL WALLIS, flautist, Australian soldier who participated in the war and was killed in the White Sand Desert at the age of 33

MAI, nurse, attached to the Special Intelligence Battalion, killed in the White Sand Desert at the age of 29

AN, returned soldier, old comrade-in-arms with Lam, aged 68

QUAN, Chairman of the People's Council of the White Sand Desert, son of Lam, aged 44

PHI, soldier in the Special Intelligence Battalion, fought in the White Sand Desert, aged 30

SETTING

The action of the play takes place in the White Sand Desert where many fierce battles were fought.

ACT ONE

SCENE ONE

THE WITCH OF THE WHITE SAND DESERT

A vast white sand desert spreads out to the horizon. Barbwire fences surrounding the old military compound, left over from the war, stand out as spiky black lines against the glaring white sand, under the scorching sun. Pointing to the military compound is an old, bleached, wooden board in the shape of an arrow. On it is written: 'Danger! Keep Out! Landmines!' The sign is nailed on the trunk of a large tree whose exposed roots resemble giant Komodo dragons sun baking. Near the tree lies an old burnt-out tank whose gun points straight to the sky. The sinister squawking sound of crows can be heard. The shadows of two figures in white shrouds appear and disappear near the tree.

QUAN and MARY are sitting in the shade of the tree, studying geographical names on a map spread out in front of them.

QUAN: [*looking up, his eyes following the flight of the crows*] The war ended decades ago and still the smell of death hangs in the air. [*Pointing to the burnt-out tank*] That tank. It was destroyed by my father. Shot and burned. A few years ago, he would bring the children here and tell them stories of his heroic deeds. But now he's an old sick man. And children these days find games more interesting than war stories. But also they are scared to come.

MARY: Scared?

QUAN: They are scared of the Crone.

MARY: The woman everyone avoids?

QUAN: Yes. People call her the 'Witch of the White Sand Desert', and use her to frighten children into being good. She lives here.

MARY: In that tank?

QUAN: Apparently she calls it the 'Castle of the Dead Souls'. The boys who spy on her say she avoids talking to anyone real. It's as if she is afraid of the living.

MARY: I understand why the children are scared.

QUAN: Unfortunately she is the only person who knows this desert. She's walked every path, seen every corner. The only way to get through it is with her. If she'll take you. [*Pause.*] Are you sure this is where your father died?

MARY: His friend gave me this map. It shows where he was killed.

QUAN: [*examining the map carefully*] According to this… here's the fence, that's the fort… that barbwire area over there is where the battle took place. I'm afraid the movement of the sand over the years has covered everything.

MARY: What's that spot where the crows are landing?

QUAN: It used to be one of the most important postings during the war. Many people died there.

MARY: That's where I'll start looking.

QUAN: Impossible! The compound is full of landmines.

MARY: Can I get a mine detector?

QUAN: It's pointless. We've tried to clear it many times before. But it's too dangerous without modern equipment and we're just too poor. Feeding hungry people is more important.

MARY: Is there any other way? I can pay.

QUAN: A few years ago, an American family came here wanting to recover the remains of their relatives. They offered a huge sum of money and our people are very poor. But no one would accept the offer. That's how dangerous it is.

MARY: So no one dares go inside?

QUAN: Perhaps only the crows. And the Crone. The locals say she goes in there. Digging for bones.

MARY: Has she found anything?

QUAN: No one knows. Every now and then we hear a mine go off and we think the Crone's been killed. But then, after a few days, people see her again, wandering the sand dunes. It seems she's protected by the souls of the dead.

MARY: Is this tree also protected by the dead? It seems to be the only living thing around here.

QUAN: I don't know. It's been here since the war.

MARY: Were you here then?

QUAN: No, I was studying in the Soviet Union. When I came back, the war was over. And here in the middle of the desert was this tree. No one knows who planted it. The superstitious locals believe God granted them the tree because they had suffered such a harsh life. The tree gives them hope.

MARY: This place has so many stories.

QUAN: My father knows them all. He was honoured as a hero, awarded many medals. I told him you were coming and he urged me to help you. He also said to invite you to a traditional ceremony we're having. It's the anniversary of my grandparents' death. We cook a special meal and offer some to the gods.

MARY: That's wonderful. I'd love to come.

QUAN: He'll be pleased to meet you. I should tell you his face was badly burned during the war. [*Looking at his watch*] It's time we got back.

MARY: I think… maybe… I should stay.

QUAN: The Crone is not exactly normal.

MARY: I need to meet her. I will stay.

QUAN: [*offering her his mobile phone*] Please take this phone, so we can keep in contact. If you have any problems please call me.

MARY: [*taking the phone from* QUAN] Thank you. You've been a great help.

QUAN: Good luck! Be careful.

MARY: I will.

> QUAN *exits quickly.* MARY *is alone. Time passes. The* CRONE *enters. She is an old decrepit woman in rags, her scraggy hair falling over her dark, haggy eyes which look like two deep, dark holes in her wrinkled face. On her bent back she carries an old, rusty hoe and a heavy, dirty, tattered bag. She drags her bare feet slowly across the hot sand. She stops at the tree and puts her load down. She sits wearily against the tree trunk. She wipes the sweat from her face with the front of her shirt.*

CRONE: Nothing here worth taking. The sand will bury you tonight.

MARY: Good afternoon. I want… may I ask you a question?

CRONE: I don't know how to answer.

MARY: Please. Don't run away! I have to talk to you. Please, Crone…

CRONE: How come you know what I'm called?

MARY: I've heard about this place. I was hoping you'd show me the safe way to cross the desert.

CRONE: If the sand lets you live, you'll live.

> *She pours out the contents of her bag—skulls, an assortment of old bones—then calmly, using the front of her shirt, lovingly polishes each bone.*

MARY: Did you find these bones in there?

CRONE: Would you be knowing someone among them?

MARY: My father died here… during the war.

CRONE: Why come again?

MARY: I want to find his remains.

CRONE: Once upon a time, there were long-legged creatures who came and dropped fire on short-legged creatures. [*Singing*] La… la… la… Find the short or the long bones?

MARY: Bones… bones…

CRONE: Long bones!

MARY: How do you know?

CRONE: The dead souls tell me. [*Caressing the bones*] Go away now! I have to feed my babies!

MARY: Please let me stay. I'll help you polish the bones.

CRONE: [*throwing a leg bone over to* MARY] Hey, long-legged whitey. People call these human bones. But I don't. What do you call them?

> MARY *slowly picks up some bones, then uses the front of her shirt to polish them as the* CRONE *does.*

MARY: What else could we call them? They're human bones.

CRONE: No one can see anything.

MARY: What do you call them then?

CRONE: Human bones.

MARY: What are you going to do with them?

CRONE: I use them to beat up those who killed my children. The sand is free to dance with the wind but they were not free to enjoy their lives.

> *The* CRONE *threatens* MARY *with a bone.*

MARY: Please. I didn't kill them.

> *The* CRONE *walks away.*

CRONE: Come here.

MARY: You won't hit me?

CRONE: The Crone does not make any promises. [*Pause.*] This is the head of my eldest son. Such an intelligent boy. [*Throwing the skull*] You ungrateful son!

She sings.

I am the autumn leaves,
You are the spring leaves!
Why did you fall from the branch earlier than me!

MARY *and the* CRONE *are alone in the desert. Time passes.* AN *runs in, a bottle of water and a bag of food in his hand.*

AN: Hi, Crone! Here's some food and water! Sorry I'm late, the wind's coming up fast.

CRONE: I told that long-legged whitey to go, otherwise she'll be buried.

AN: Who are you? Why are you here?

MARY: I'm—

AN: Listen. The Crone is right. A big sandstorm is coming. You'd better go now.

MARY: The local radio station didn't say anything about a storm.

AN: Don't believe the radio here. Just take a look at the horizon. In a few minutes the whole desert will be buried.

CRONE: [*singing*]
I throw the sand to the sky
to create a screen protecting my children
from burning in the sun…!

MARY: [*while the* CRONE *sings*] What is the Crone singing? I don't understand!

The CRONE *continues to sing under the conversation which follows.*

CRONE: [*singing*]
… blow up the wind to create a storm
to break the wings of the crows
stopping them
picking at the bones
of my children!
Hey, nasty crows!
Watch out!

You can't eat my children!
La… la… la…!
The wind carries the sand far away!
I am calling the souls of my children back to dinner!

AN: She is calling her children back for dinner. Don't worry. The song doesn't mean anything to a tourist.

MARY: I'm not a tourist.

AN: How come you can speak the local language so well?

MARY: I studied. I've come to look for my father's remains.

AN: Have you found them?

MARY: Not yet! I only started today. I think he may have died in the compound. The Chairman of the local council told me there were battles in there.

AN: That's right. I fought in those battles. [*Pause.*] The name of the person who told you is Mr Quan. Is that right?

MARY: You know him?

AN: Every now and then Mr Quan organises meetings to inform us of new decisions of the Communist Party. So we all know him.

MARY: His father is a war hero.

AN: [*laughing*] Yes. A war hero. We were close friends. We were children.

MARY: Why are you laughing? Is there something funny?

CRONE: My children are not like this. They are flesh and blood.

AN: I find the Crone kicking a skull funny.

MARY: I need to look inside the compound.

AN: No…

MARY: Would you help me?

AN: … it's too dangerous—

MARY: Please. I can pay.

AN: [*laughing*] I am afraid of having lots of money. I am used to living in poverty. I couldn't bear the happiness that money is supposed to bring!

MARY: Are you a friend of the Crone?

AN: People avoid her because they are scared of her madness! I try to stay close to her because I have nothing left to lose! A crazy friend is better than none.

MARY: I need her to help me through the desert.

AN: There's no way. The only roads are made when people walk on the sand. But the wind and the sand cover the footprints immediately.

MARY: You fought in there. Did you see any white soldiers die?

AN: Many. I picked up a few things that belonged to them. I could show you. They're at my home. It's not far from here.

MARY: Great. Can we go now?

AN: No… the storm. The sand will bury alive anything that steps into it. I was born here, I have seen many people buried.

MARY: Is there a safe place near by?

CRONE: Is there a safe place anywhere?

AN: Let me ask the Crone's permission for us to stay inside the tank.

CRONE: [*standing in* MARY*'s way*] Hey, long-legged whitey! You are not to enter the Castle of the Dead Souls.

> *The sky turns dark. The wind hisses. The mobile phone placed next to* MARY*'s backpack rings loudly.* MARY *runs towards it, but the* CRONE *is faster and she snatches it. She pushes a button on the phone and sings loudly into it.* MARY *tries to catch her but she keeps on running, dancing around and singing.*

[*Singing*] La… la… la…
I throw the sand to the sky
to create a screen to protect my children
from burning in the sun!
I blow up the wind to create
a storm to break the wings
of the crows stopping them from
picking at the bones of my children!
Hey, nasty crows! Watch out!

> *The* CRONE *throws the phone into the sand.*

You can't eat my children!
La… la… la…!
The wind carries the sand far away!
I am calling the souls of my children back for dinner!

MARY: [*over the singing*] Please give me back the phone. Please tell her to give me my phone back.

AN: [*running to hold* MARY *back*] You see the big sand dunes collapsing? It's gone! Don't risk your life looking for it!

MARY: [*angrily*] The phone's not mine. The Chairman lent it to me. [*Jumping into the sand hole and calling out*] Jesus! It is so dark in here. I can't see a thing.

CRONE: The more you look, the harder it is to find!

AN: Stop looking! Come back up! No one can tell which sand dune will collapse next.

MARY: Did you see which direction she threw the phone?

CRONE: I threw it in the direction of the caller!

AN: Be careful! The sand dune behind is collapsing! Get out now! The sand is falling in! Get out!

> *It looks as if the sand is pouring into the hole where* MARY *is looking.* MARY*'s call for help can be heard.* AN, *desperate, takes a hoe and jumps in to save* MARY.

[*Yelling from below*] Crone! Come and help me get her out!

CRONE: I am not helping the people who killed my children.

AN: [*yelling again*] Come and help me pull her up!

CRONE: [*not moving*] I am not helping people who killed my children.

AN: [*screaming from below*] Please hurry up! The sand's up to our knees already.

CRONE: I am not helping people who killed my children!

AN: [*screaming desperately*] If she dies it is because of you, Crone! You will be blamed for your cruelty.

CRONE: [*walking towards the hole*] I am not cruel!

AN: Please! Hold my hand. We will both pull her out.

CRONE: [*stretching out her hand*] I can't reach! I can't stretch my arm any further! Throw me the hoe.

AN: [*more desperate*] It's under the sand.

> *The* CRONE *looks around, finds a leg bone and holds it out to* AN.

CRONE: Hold on to the bone!

AN: [*yelling loudly*] Pull now!

> *The* CRONE *pulls hard, then suddenly lets go of the bone.*

[*Yelling*] Why did you let go?

CRONE: You climb up yourself. Leave the whitey! When my children were bombed, no one helped them.

AN: [*screaming louder*] If you don't, I'll stay down here and die with her. [*Throwing the bone back up*] No one will come to see you! You will be completely alone.

> *The* CRONE *hesitates for a moment, then picks up the bone and holds it out to* AN *again.*

CRONE: Hold the bone, I will pull you out. There, hold the bone. I will let the Whitey stay in my children's castle. Hold the bone tight, I'll pull.

She pulls with all her might. AN *holds the bone with one hand and with the other he tries to pull* MARY. *Slowly he crawls out of the hole pulling* MARY *up.* MARY *lies unconscious on the roots of the tree. The wind blows furiously, spreading sand everywhere.* AN *pours some water on* MARY*'s face to revive her. Further away, the* CRONE *stands on the tank with a burning torch in one hand, throwing sand in the air, singing.*

[*Singing*] La… la… la…
I throw the sand to the sky
to create a sun screen
protecting my children from burning
in the sun!
I blow up the wind to create
a storm to break the wings
of the crows stopping them from
picking at the bones of my children!
Hey, nasty crows! Watch out!
You can't eat my children!
La… la… la…!
The wind carries the sand far away!
I am calling the souls of my children back for dinner!

The shadows of the two figures in white shrouds move in time with the CRONE*'s singing, blending into the howling wind.*

SCENE TWO

THE CASTLE OF THE DEAD SOULS

Night. The desert. The storm rages. Inside the narrow driver's compartment of the burnt-out tank, MARY *lies unconscious.* AN *squeezes the last drop of water into her mouth. The* CRONE *lights up a kerosene lamp and crawls into a corner of the compartment, quickly praying, rhythmically beating two bones together. The shadows of the two figures in white shrouds move gently around the tree. The bones collected by the* CRONE *are hung all around the tank compartment. They sway to and fro. The different tones of the voices of the dead souls blend with the sound of the howling wind and the rhythmic tapping of the* CRONE. MARY *wakes up, puzzled. She looks at the bones.*

MARY: Where am I?

AN: You are in the 'Castle of the Dead Souls'.

MARY: Whose bones are they? They look at me with their red eyes… as if from Hell.

AN: [*reaching up to gently touch the bones*] They are the Crone's. Every bone she finds she brings back here, cleans it up and then hangs it up. Don't be afraid. They were once living souls like us.

MARY: I can only see bones.

    Voices of the dead souls can be heard.

I can hear somebody calling my name [*Listening carefully*] My father. It's his voice. He's around here somewhere.

AN: It's only the wind.

MARY: No. It's my father calling. For me. Hear that. It is very, very near. He is floating just above us. Or is it under the sand? [*Calling out*] Dad! Dad! I'm here. Can you hear me? Where are you? I thought I saw your shadow just then!

AN: You are haunted by him.

    Pause.

MARY: Did I faint?

AN: You had a long sleep.

MARY: It's so dark! Where's the sun?

AN: I'm afraid the sun was hopelessly drunk and was carried away by the storm.

MARY: What time is it?

AN: The castle has no time. Only an old, crazy mother who sits every night next to the bones of her children.

MARY: Did the war happen right here?

AN: Yes, right here. Such a long time since we had a violent storm like this. A sandstorm in a time of peace.

MARY: Why is the Crone making those sounds?

AN: Saying prayers.

MARY: Does she pray all night?

AN: No, she sleeps and the prayers are her lullaby.

MARY: Who does she pray for?

AN: For the dead as well as for the living.

MARY: When will she wake up?

AN: You'll know, she will be singing or crying.

MARY: I'm very thirsty, could I have a drink?

AN: I gave you the last drop. Just wait till the storm calms down, I'll fetch you some water.

MARY: Doesn't the Crone have any?

AN: Perhaps she drinks her own tears.

MARY: Such a storm and no rain.

AN: Here it rains only sand.

> *A long silence.* MARY *sits up.* AN *smiles at her.*

MARY: You have such a sad smile.

AN: A lot of people smile but it doesn't mean they're happy.

> *Silence, except for the diminishing voices of the dead souls and the regular sound of the tapping of bones by the* CRONE. *The storm abates. Outside the tank,* QUAN *with a torch, bare-headed, is searching and calling for* MARY. *He climbs on top of the tank for a better view. Overhearing the voices inside the tank, he crouches down, putting his ear against the tank and listening carefully to the conversation.*

MARY: I hope Mr Quan isn't worried about me. Are you still friends with his father?

AN: There were three of us. Every day we played together in the sand dunes. Our hopes soared as high as the kites we flew. The War Hero used to make beautiful kites. I would play my bamboo flute while the girl sang. Her singing was as beautiful as she was. All the men said she was such a rare pearl in this harsh land.

MARY: Who was she?

AN: It's a dream that's over. [*Pause.*] I wanted to be a poet, he wanted to be a famous hero and she wanted to be a singer.

> *He hears a traditional song.*

[*Looking happier*] Listen, do you hear it? She's singing a song about eternal love.

MARY: You look much happier when you remember her singing.

AN: [*cheering up*] We used to ask her if she sang for a special person? Her answer was: 'None of your business! You don't need to know for whom I sing!' I teased her: 'If there is a singer then there must be a listener.' She replied cheekily: 'Whoever wants to listen can hear my songs.' The War Hero said: 'But everyone loves your singing.' She smiled: 'Even so, I only sing for one person.' We both asked her: 'Who is this lucky person?' and she answered shyly: 'The person I love.'

MARY: Who was it?

AN: One day, my friend the Hero was flying his kite. He said: 'Whoever she loves is a happy man!' My reply was: 'It's you. Who else could it be? Whenever she sings, she's always glancing at you!' But he told me: 'You're more suitable. You accompany her with your bamboo flute. I've met her several times down by the river and all she talked about was you.' I said: 'No. Your family has land, buffaloes and orchards. I am very poor, I don't think she's interested in me.' He gave me a big thump on my back, laughing: 'I will donate my wealth to support your love. Love is not for me! All I want is to be a hero!' He dragged me to see her to find out if she loved me. She nodded her head as her answer, and then ran into the sand dunes far into the horizon, leaving behind her a beautiful red glow of the afternoon.

MARY: Where is she now?

AN: Maybe she is somewhere around here.

> *A long silence.*

> *The hanging bones swing to and fro according to the different tones of the voices of the dead souls.*

MARY: [*in a soft voice*] Did you love her very much?

AN: [*trying to be cheerful*] We promised to be faithful to each other forever, just like the words in her song. But then, in 1954, the Land Reform Movement began here, in the White Sand Desert—where there's not much land to reform, but plenty of sand. Oh God! People are so cruel! I cursed that Land Reform Movement. It turned my friend from a kite-maker into a cruel monster. The locals are only interested in talking about their victorious war. They have forgotten that behind the medals of the War Hero lie countless sufferings.

MARY: Mr Quan told me you haven't seen his father since the war. What happened?

AN: How can I tell you? He caused so much pain.

The warm voice of a girl singing can be heard.

Do you hear the singing? She is singing! She sings about eternal love! The song is still here but the singer was… the War Hero…

MARY: What happened to them?

AN: My friend the Hero denounced his father in front of the Land Reform Committee. He claimed his father was a mean landowner who ripped off the peasants and that he owned a buffalo, a couple acres of land and a silver tea set. So the peasant revolutionaries dragged his father out to the field, tied him up and left him there to die under the hot sun. The son was rewarded for being an example of the Land Reform Movement and a hero of the class struggle! His wife hanged herself that night—in the same field where her son was declared a hero! The War Hero with the half-burnt face. The model citizen of the White Sand Desert.

QUAN *bursts into the compartment. The* CRONE *wakes up frightened. She holds on to the clanking bone.*

QUAN: What right have you to dishonour my father in front of a stranger?

MARY: Mr Quan!

QUAN: My father told me my grandparents sacrificed themselves for the most bitter class struggle. My father himself fought heroically in the war, his name was associated with many victories. Everyone respects and admires him. You're lying.

AN: And what if what I said is true?

QUAN: Then I will have to force my father to go before the People of the White Sand Desert and tell them what he really did.

AN: [*bursting out laughing*] Confessions of a war hero?

QUAN: [*seriously*] We are struggling for a fair and just society here in the White Sand Desert. I swear to bring into the open any person who committed any crime, even if that person happens to be my father!

AN: [*laughing shockingly*] You sound exactly like your father—you weren't even born then. So there, my dear young Communist! Do you want people to drag your father out and leave him to die under the hot sun, just like your grandfather before him? Don't believe me. It's only the story of a crazed old man, confused in a furious night's sandstorm.

MARY: In my country, on April Fool's Day, everyone is allowed to play whatever tricks they like. Perhaps, Mr Quan, we could consider tonight as a Fools' night.

QUAN: [*to* AN] I will personally check with my father about your story!

AN: Don't!

QUAN: Why?

AN: Everyone in the White Sand Desert puts their faith in your father! Here, in this sandy place, there are people who were born and died for such a faith. What will happen to them if they lose it? The meat party of the war is over, only white bones remain. Sooner or later the sorrow caused by the party will be buried in memories. [*Listening*] The storm's finishing. Listen to the gentle wind on the dunes. Let's leave children to grow and fly kites and sing and believe in heroes.

> QUAN *goes to leave.*

MARY: Mr Quan! Wait for me! Let me go with you!

> QUAN *quickly climbs up to get out of the tank.* MARY *follows him out.* AN *stands motionless like a statue. The* CRONE *caresses the bones and starts singing. Her warm and tender voice blends harmoniously with the sound of the wind and the voices of the dead souls.*

CRONE: [*singing*]
> The storm is over!
> Please come and eat, my children!
> The rice is from the dried fields of this desert,
> the fish is from the dried-out rivers of this region!
> My love for you is as vast as the sunshine over the sand dunes!
> Eat, my children, please eat, my children…!

> *The shadows of the two figures in white shrouds move around each other while the* CRONE *sings.*

SCENE THREE

THE HERO WHO WANTS TO GO TO HELL

Lam's house, prepared for the anniversary celebration of Quan's grandparents' death. In the middle of the room is a table groaning with sumptuous food. A large, framed portrait of Lenin hangs on the wall. Below it, a portrait of Quan's grandparents in traditional head dress and costumes. A doorway under the two portraits leads to the back room of the house. The shadows of the two figures in white shrouds walk around the room invisible to both QUAN *and* LAM. *A small radio sits in a corner of the room playing an international Communist song.* MARY *and* QUAN *sit impatiently in silence waiting for* LAM *at the table. After a while,* QUAN *walks over to turn down the volume of the radio then stops at the doorway, where he calls out to his father.*

QUAN: Excuse me, Father! Our guest is here, why don't you come and join us.

LAM: [*from the back room*] Please tell the visitor I am coming.

QUAN: [*to* MARY] Whenever we have foreign visitors he plans every last detail. [*Joyfully*] So… what are your impressions of the White Sand Desert?

MARY: It is as I imagined, a typical desert with…

> LAM *in a carefully pressed suit, wearing rows of medals, appears at the doorway. Half of his face is scarred from burns and he carries a beautiful red paper kite.*

LAM: [*quickly completing* MARY*'s sentence*] … with a tradition of famous heroic and revolutionary deeds. I have the honour of representing all the revolutionaries of the White Sand Desert in welcoming you.

MARY: I am honoured to meet you!

LAM: [*proffering the kite to* MARY] This red kite is the symbol of the victorious Revolution of the White Sand Desert—red symbolises both the blood sacrificed by so many for freedom and the triumphant history of the proletarian Revolution.

MARY: It's a beautiful kite! Thank you so much.

LAM: My pleasure! Should you have any wishes, this kite will carry them up to the sky and they will be granted.

MARY: My only wish is to find my father's remains.

LAM: Searching for the soul is much more difficult than finding bones. [*To* QUAN, *quickly*] I told you to put some chilli sauce in the beef stir-fry—did you?

QUAN: I did exactly as you instructed me.

LAM: Good! [*Looking over the other dishes*] The preparation for today's anniversary of your grandparents' passing is excellent. [*To* MARY] This is the same everyday food—vegetables and meat—but it is the art in the cooking which gives it the spiritual flavour of the Revolution. Please, have some chicken and mushroom. [*He turns to* QUAN.] Was this chicken given to me by the Returned Soldiers League?

QUAN: No, we ate that last week. This chicken was given to us by the White Sand Desert Collective Group of the Red Flag Youth.

MARY: Really?

LAM: They raise them for the family of the revolutionaries—especially.

MARY: Yummy!

LAM: [*to* MARY] The fact that the youth know how to raise chickens to feed old soldiers reflects the spirit and tradition of the proletarian Revolution in the White Sand Desert. Do you find the chicken better here than in Australia?

MARY: Australian chickens are not raised in the spirit of revolution so maybe their taste isn't as good!

QUAN: Please, Father! Mary is a very famous musician in Australia.

LAM: [*clapping his hands noisily*] I knew it! The way you speak so melodically. Do you come from a family of musicians?

MARY: Both my grandfather and father were musicians. Unfortunately, my father's musical career was cut short.

LAM: Perhaps you will continue it. [*Pointing to* QUAN] I am very proud that my son has inherited our spirit of revolutionary tradition.

QUAN: Please, Father, try a glass of Mary's wine. She brought it from Australia.

MARY: I hope you like it.

> LAM *takes the glass, examines it carefully, then returns it to* QUAN.

LAM: I must make it clear to you before I drink, that wine and revolutionary ideal do not mix! The Party and the People would never forgive anyone who lets wine weaken the determination and the will to build a truly successful Socialist society. Do you understand?

QUAN: Yes, Father. I understood everything you have taught me.

LAM: Good! Excellent! The more you understand the better you will be! [*Turning to* MARY] I've always trained my son not to neglect his duties by bowing to mere pleasures.

MARY: You can be proud of your son! [*Looking at* LAM*'s medals*] You have been awarded so many medals. Does each of these represent a victory?

LAM: [*chewing his food gluttonously, looking down at this chest*] Yes, and there are lots more. There isn't enough room on my whole body to wear all my medals. Today, I wear only the highest. I have a drawer full of medals and commendations! Let me show you!

QUAN: Please, Father. The beef and chilli and lemon grass stir-fry is getting cold.

LAM: [*putting some beef in* MARY*'s bowl*] You're right. Please have a taste of this. It's a speciality of this region.

QUAN: Medals and commendations don't get cold, but beef with chilli and lemon grass is tasteless when it is cold.

LAM: I don't like it when you compare my medals with food!

QUAN: I am sorry, Father! I spoke without thinking. Please forgive me.

MARY: [*tasting some beef*] This is really delicious.

> LAM *picks up a piece of beef and shows it to* QUAN.

LAM: [*in seriousness*] As you are the Chairman of the People's Council of the White Sand Desert, I'd like to hear your comments on this piece of meat.

MARY: I think it is very tasty.

QUAN: Yes, Father. I didn't find anything wrong with it.

LAM: A true Communist will never stop training and tuning his five senses to even the smallest details he experiences in daily life. Details to which others would be oblivious. He then can easily identify the important and complex problems in his revolutionary missions.

QUAN: Yes, Father. I am ready for your instruction.

LAM: Just look at this piece of meat, you can see that the cattle are not well fed! You would do well to remind the directors of the cattle co-operative to take more care of their herd.

QUAN: Yes, Father, tomorrow I will convene a meeting to address the matter. The subject will be 'the future of our cattle'.

LAM: I approve your concern and practical response to my suggestion!

MARY: You are amazing!

LAM: You need a keen sense of awareness and perception to be able to carry out three revolutions at once: there is the Revolution of Production…

QUAN: Excuse me, Father!

LAM: How many times have I told you not to interrupt when I am speaking?! We struggle hard for a free democratic society. I always encourage you to formulate well-founded opinions but they must be expressed with discipline and within the approved framework of the ideology. [*To* MARY] Where was I?

MARY: You were talking about the Revolution of Production.

LAM: Quite right! And there is the Revolution of Science and there is the Revolution of Thought. [*To* QUAN] I have said my piece, now you may speak.

QUAN: Please, Father. I only wish to offer you a toothpick, there is a piece of chicken stuck in between your teeth.

LAM: [*quickly covering his mouth and picking his teeth*] This is a meat party. Everyone at a meat party will get scraps stuck in their teeth. It's inevitable.

    A long silence.

MARY: [*looking up at the photograph of* QUAN*'s grandparents*] Your parents look very gentle.

LAM: Yes, they both were martyrs of the White Sand Desert.

QUAN: [*to* MARY] See. I told that crazy old man. [*To* LAM] He said my grandfather was left to die under the hot sun and my grandmother hanged herself. I told him it wasn't true.

    A long silence.

LAM: Haven't I told you time and time again that everyone has the right to say what they think?! Society is like a chicken coop. Not every hen lays its eggs at our will! A true Communist must always remember that our duty is to serve the People! Our diplomatic approach is a useful instrument in assuring those who say we are their enemy that, in fact, we are not. Your hot headedness is of no use.

QUAN: Yes, Father. I understand what you say. But how can I remain calm when that crazy old man dishonoured you in front of such a famous musician as Mary here? And I can't imagine he was ever a friend of yours.

LAM: A true Communist can befriend anyone. [*Pause.*] Where does he live now?

MARY: In a tent, near the desert.

LAM: How could you let your people live in such squalor?

QUAN: Please, Father. I have to face thousands of problems. How to stop my people from starving. How to improve our communication network. How to prevent sandstorms from destroying our rice fields. Defeating illiteracy. Provisions for health services. Eradicating social ills. I carry on my shoulder the responsibilities for a better future of the entire population in this region. I have no time to concern myself with one crazy old man. I just don't understand him.

LAM: How can you care for the entire population when you can't even understand just one person?

QUAN: Please, Father.

LAM: Don't talk back. You are shaming me in front of our foreign friend with your so-called leadership! A true Communist should know how to look after his people as he would look after the pupil of his own eye! You'd better grant the old man a housing permit, first thing tomorrow.

QUAN: Providing a house for a person who dishonoured you? In my opinion Socialism has no room for such a person!

LAM: Your duty is to help people like him to change—spiritually and physically—even if it costs you your life. [*Pause.*] Let me ask you this: if you are to die for the Revolution in this desert, would you like to go to Heaven or to Hell?

QUAN: Dear Father, my spirit would go wherever the Revolution guides me!

LAM *nods approvingly.*

MARY: Which would you choose, Mr Lam? Heaven or Hell?

LAM: Hell.

MARY: Why?

LAM: If I didn't go to Hell there would be no one to enlighten those people who accused me of doing despicable deeds!

MARY: We foreigners really need to understand you better.

QUAN: [*to* LAM] Some foreign antique dealers are in town. They said they're interested in buying your old war uniforms, the portrait of Lenin and all your war medals.

LAM: Why didn't you spit in their faces for my sake?! [*He stands up quickly and walks over to the portrait of Lenin.*] Dear Lenin! You are the guiding light in the heart of every Communist in the world! How dare those small insects dare to consider your portrait as a commercial commodity? [*Suddenly turning to* MARY] Have you read the complete works of Lenin?

MARY: I've been busy with my music, I haven't had time to read Lenin's work. I also confess I'm not much good at politics, I prefer the arts.

LAM: Politics is an art! You should read Lenin on Socialism. His books are excellent! I remember his quote 'Socialism manifests through the government of the soviets and the total electrification of a nation'.

    The room plunges into darkness due to the shortage of electricity. MARY *laughs.*

QUAN: [*in the darkness*] Problems with the generators again! My apologies to you, Mary. Please bear with me for a moment while I light the kerosene lamp.

MARY: It doesn't matter. We can still talk in the dark!

LAM: [*speaking loudly in the darkness*] We have achieved the most important part: we already are governed by the soviets! [*To* QUAN] Where did you hide the lamp? Why does it take you so long to find it? Electricity shortage is just a temporary problem. Soon, Lenin's word will be completely realised in the White Sand Desert!

MARY: The Russians have demolished all the statues of Lenin?

QUAN: Please, Mary! Don't talk about it.

LAM: Why not? I believe it is done by the hands of the international reactionaries and their cohorts. Have the true Russian Communists rebuilt them yet?

MARY: Don't you know? It was the members of the Russian Communist Party themselves who demolished the statues.

QUAN: Excuse me, Mary! I have asked you not to mention that news
   here.

   Pause.

MARY: I am sorry. But I thought the whole world already knew about it!
LAM: Quan! Is it true what she just said?
QUAN: Yes, father, it is the truth!
LAM: Why did you hide it from me?
QUAN: I was afraid the news would upset you.

   A long silence.

LAM: [*yelling out*] Where is the lamp? Why does it take you so long to
   find it?

   *Suddenly voices of the dead souls can be heard. Then skeletons,
   with candles inside their rib cages, float down into the room.
   The skeletons land and walk around the room as if they are
   shadows of people with hearts exposed and beating.* LAM *stands,
   shaking with terror.*

[*Looking at the skeletons*] Who are you? Please leave my house!
MARY: Are you all right, Mr Lam?
QUAN: Excuse me, Father! Are you talking to someone?
LAM: Can't you see? The skeletons are walking around in the room!
   There, you see, they are walking. There—
MARY: Sorry, I can't see a thing!
LAM: [*yelling*] There, you see over there, the skeletons are coming towards
   me! Tell them to go away! Their red eyes are staring! Go away! What
   do you want? Quan! Where is the lamp? Light the lamp quickly!

   LAM *is terrified. He covers his head with his hands and slumps
   down. The skeletons disappear quickly.* QUAN *lights the large lamp.
   The room is inundated with bright light.*

QUAN: [*going to his father*] Father! Who were you talking to?
LAM: The skeletons. Where have they gone?
QUAN: I'm sorry, Father! I didn't see anything.

   A very long silence.

LAM: Are the Communists still in power in Russia?
QUAN: Please, Father! Don't bother about that old history. You are tired.
   Let Mary play us a piece of music. It will help you relax.

MARY: [*taking out the flute from her backpack*] This piece of music was written by my grandfather when he was young. I learned it from my father when I was a child. It's my only inheritance. Now it is my turn to teach my own children to play it.

LAM: Do you also play the flute?

MARY: Every member of my family plays it.

QUAN: Please play.

> MARY *raises the flute to her lips. Music emits from the flute suddenly—a beautiful and sad tune.* QUAN *listens to the flute attentively.* LAM *looks at* MARY *dazed, acting as if he has just seen something frightening come out of the sound of the flute. All of a sudden the space is glowing in a bright red colour, with voices of people screaming and the sounds of bombs and gunfire. All blend together with* MARY*'s flute playing.* LAM *stands up slowly, his head in his hands, and staggers towards the other back room.* QUAN *runs to him, trying to catch him as he falls down.* MARY *stops playing.*

[*Anxiously*] Father! Father! What's happened?

LAM: Tell that woman to leave immediately! I want her out of the White Sand Desert now.

QUAN: [*bewildered*] Please, Father! What's wrong?

LAM: I want her to leave! Do you hear me?

QUAN: Yes, Father! But it was you who agreed to help. You said it was all right for me to help her.

MARY: I'm sorry. I didn't mean to do anything wrong.

LAM: Now is not the right time for you to look for your father's remains. Perhaps some other time, in the future, we will be in a better position to offer you assistance.

MARY: Please! The image of my father is part of me. I've worked very hard for this trip. I have been dreaming about it for so many years. To come here. To find his remains. To find that part of myself. Please, Mr Quan, please let me stay.

QUAN: I am sorry, but I can't go against my father's orders.

MARY: Why? I haven't done anything. At least give me a reason. All I've done is play a piece of music.

LAM: There are simply too many landmines in the desert. We don't want you getting hurt.

MARY: Mr Quan! Please help me to change your father's mind, please?

> LAM *angrily pushes the table over, the plates of food are scattered all over the floor.*

LAM: I have spoken. *No* is *no!*

> *They all stand motionless in an intense silence. The shadows of the two figures in white shrouds appear then disappear in the middle of the room.*

END OF ACT ONE

ACT TWO

SCENE ONE

TREASURE CHEST OF THE DEPARTED SOLDIERS

An's dilapidated hut. The roof is made of an old tarpaulin used by the Americans during the war. There is hardly any furniture except for an old bamboo bed, a used ammunition box for a table and two old cannon shells placed upside down for seats.

Late afternoon. The last glow of sunlight gives the sand dunes far into the distance a bright red hue. A bowl with incense is burning on the ammunition box, the smoke floating in front of a small photograph framed carefully under glass. It is the picture of a beautiful young girl. In the right corner, a few bamboo flutes and some half-made straw hats sit on a small shelf. The shadows of the two figures in white shrouds appear and disappear outside. MARY, *puzzled, looks at the simple abode.* AN *carries one of the cannon shells and places it in front of* MARY. AN *drinks throughout the scene.*

MARY: I've come to say goodbye. And to thank you.

AN: You're leaving?

MARY: Tomorrow night.

AN: Why?

MARY: They said it's because of the landmines, but I think there must be other reasons. If it was only the mines, they wouldn't have agreed to my coming in the first place. But what can I do? [*Pause.*] They told me they're giving you a new house.

AN: Yes. I said no. [*Pause.*] Would you like some rice brandy?

MARY: No thanks. Are you going to stay in this… hut… forever?

AN: I'd like to live in a proper house. But I have a fear. Living in the White Sand Desert has taught me about fear. In this life nothing is free. [*Pause.*] Will you come back again?

MARY: I don't think I'll get another chance. This is it. You said you picked up a few things from the dead white soldiers. Could we look at them? Maybe I'll find something there and my trip won't have been wasted.

AN: I keep them in this ammunition box. We will wait for the incense to finish burning. Then we'll look.

MARY: The smell of the incense is beautiful and strange. Like it's part of some separate world.

AN: Every time I want to look at the belongings of the dead white soldiers, I have to ask their permission by offering them incense. Excuse me. [*Pointing to the cannon shell*] Please sit down! Don't be afraid, the war is over. It is only an empty shell!

MARY: Do you use them as chairs?

AN: [*smiling gently*] Yes, I sit on them and think to myself during the war, one single shell can kill a lot of people, and in the time of peace, it can only sit one person!

MARY: Wow! This is the first time I've sat on one of these.

AN: How does it feel?

MARY: Cold. I imagine they all do. [*Pause.*] Do you really live here on your own?

AN: [*pointing to the photo of the young girl*] I have her picture, two empty cannon shells, a large ammunition box full of old things, my bamboo flute, I weave straw hats for a living, and the Crone is my good friend. That's all a person needs to live in this desert.

MARY: I keep thinking about the Crone and the dead soldiers' bones.

AN: Today she found the skeletons of a mother and two children!

A long silence.

MARY: May I have some of that brandy now?

AN: Certainly.

AN *pours.*

MARY: Perhaps you are right. The war was just a meat party. A meaningless meat party which left nothing for the next generation. Except bleached bones.

Pause.

AN: The brandy is full of sorrows.

MARY: [*looking at the photo*] Is that the girl you told me about?

AN: Yes.

MARY: She's very beautiful.

AN: Please forget that story! The incense has finished burning. Now, let me show you what's in the box.

He carefully opens up the box and pulls out some sheets of paper.

MARY: Are they your poems?

AN: 'The battle splits the moon in half.' Poems written by soldiers are to be placed at the top of the gun barrel. My poems are of no use for the proletarian Revolution of the White Sand Desert!

MARY: I don't quite understand.

AN: [*gesturing with his hands*] Don't try to. To understand is to remember! To remember is to think! And to think is to want to change what has been understood. That's why I don't want to understand anything anymore. My heart is empty. For the desert wind to fill. [*He takes out the contents from the box one by one.*] Have a look at these, you could be lucky, you might recognise something which belonged to your father.

He hands MARY *a twisted old helmet.*

This belonged to a white soldier who died right under my feet. [*He shows* MARY *one of his hands.*] This is the hand that closed those eyes. I was reprimanded in front of my whole unit for closing the eyes of a dead enemy. But once he was dead he could no longer be an enemy of anybody. [*Pause.*] Sometimes I don't know if I should laugh or cry for those days!

He brings out a handful of lighters, necklaces, fountain pens, sunglasses, handkerchiefs, name tags, rings.

Here, have a look at these. They all belonged to white soldiers!

MARY: [*examining everything*] How did you collect all this in the middle of a war?

AN: I picked them up during the quiet moments.

MARY: Some of these are very valuable.

AN: The antique dealers come here often, trying to get me to sell. I'll never agree to it. [*Drinking his wine*] They tell me that these things are very valuable, that trading will build a bridge from the desert to the outside world. Idiots! Who'd build international friendships on the belongings of dead soldiers?

He hands MARY *a singed uniform.*

Here, this uniform belonged to a red-haired soldier. He didn't run fast enough.

MARY: [*holding up a pen, examining it carefully*] This pen looks exactly like my father's.

AN: Really?

MARY: But the name isn't his. [*Sighing*] Is that all?

AN: That's it. You didn't recognise anything?

MARY: [*shaking her head*] No. Nothing here could be his. He was a musician, he lived simply. A flautist.

    A very long silence.

AN: [*avoiding* MARY*'s eyes*] A flautist?

MARY: Why are you suddenly quiet?

AN: [*avoidingly*] No… I just wanted to know—are there many flautists in your country?

MARY: Quite a few. You've knocked your cup over. Are you all right?

AN: Yes, I'm all right! Just a bit clumsy. You know old age.

MARY: Are you thinking of someone?

AN: A soldier. In war every soldier is the same. A gun, a country and an interrupted dream. [*Pause.*] Did your father play a flute very beautifully? The sound of that flute… sad as the afternoon wind on the sand dunes…

MARY: [*amazingly*] Did you meet my father? Why are you crying?

AN: [*looking out at the distant sand dunes*] No, I am not crying. I have no more tears to cry. [*Takes up his wine cup, shaking*] The rice brandy is crying! The rice brandy is angry a flautist went to war.

MARY: My mother encouraged him to go and defend Australia against the Communists. I was too young to understand what a 'Communist' was. I only knew that I missed my father and his music. My mother was very proud.

AN: The women who are left behind can only cry on one another's shoulders for their lost. [*Suddenly standing up*] That's it! Please go. There is nothing of your father's here.

MARY: I'm not sure I understand.

AN: You have seen everything I have. Please go now. You said there are many flautists in Australia.

MARY: What haven't you shown me?

AN: Nothing! I looked at you and felt sorry for you, the harsh desert has ruined your white skin.

He offers MARY *a straw hat.*

Please take this. It will remind you of this desert. Please go now. There is nothing left for you to see.

MARY: You aren't telling me the truth.

AN: [*calmly*] Truth or lie. It doesn't matter anymore. Everything is over. [*Suddenly breaking the wine cup*] Go! Go now! Get out of this White Sand Desert.

MARY: [*fearfully, looking at the broken cup*] All right! I'll go… Goodbye…

She starts to leave.

AN: [*slowly turning his head up, looking after* MARY] Excuse me!

MARY: [*stopping*] Are you calling me?

AN: Wait…

MARY: Why? You haven't got anything else to show me.

AN: [*slowly pulling a cotton first-aid bag out of the box*] I have one more thing. I do want to do the right thing by the dead souls.

MARY *turns back slowly and walks towards* AN. *He shakily pulls a twisted, singed flute from the bag.*

Please be careful, hold it gently, I don't want to lose anything of it, not even a grain of sand. There is an inscription next to the valves. Take a look, then give it back to me.

MARY, *stunned, takes the flute from* AN.

Give it back. It isn't your father's. You can go now—there's nothing else!

A very long silence.

MARY: [*shocked*] Our family will be grateful to you always!

AN: Please. Don't. I haven't done anything for you.

MARY *gently holds the flute, then slowly sits down next to* AN.

MARY: This is his. This line of writing is his name. [*Showing the valves on the flute*] This line of writing is my father's name—the flautist who died in this desert!

AN *snatches the flute back from* MARY, *then stands up and goes towards the window.*

AN: Don't play games with this old man! Pretending to be a relative of a dead soldier. Getting their belongings. So you can sell them. It's an old trick. Let the dead rest in peace. Get out.

MARY: I promise you that the flute belonged to my father.

AN: Don't make promises. A promise does not know if it can keep its own word… Solid rock can be worn down by water, so how can one expect words from the tips of people's tongues to be kept? This mouth made promises that clotted in my throat. Only silence came out. [*As if waking up from a dream, he looks around suspiciously.*] Why drink so much, you old fool? I have told myself so many times not to get so drunk.

MARY: Are you crying?

AN: They put a gun to my mouth and said they would shoot if I didn't stop crying. [*Slapping his mouth*] I swear I will never get as drunk as today! [*Slapping his mouth noisily*] Promises again! One promise caused enough miseries for a lifetime, and still more promises.

MARY *takes a photograph from her wallet and walks towards* AN.

MARY: Look here. This is the photograph of my father with his signature. It's the same as the one on the flute. My father's flute. I do not want to deceive you. How did you find this flute?

AN *looks carefully at the photo, then holds the flute close to his heart.*

Please tell me. How did you find my father's flute?

AN: [*sounding hopelessly sad*] Another sandstorm is starting.

MARY: [*walking to the door to look out*] How do you know?

AN: The whispering wind stirring up my memories.

MARY: 'The whispering wind stirring up my memories.' Is it from one of your poems?

AN: The memories are gone, only words are left. Are you really the daughter of this soldier?

MARY: Of course I am. See, I look like him.

AN: Yes, like the two grains of sand from the same desert. Each grain of sand is a heart. Each heart is a broken life. [*Sadly*] For so many decades, I've been waiting for someone to come to claim this flute.

MARY: If no one came?

AN: Then I'd take this bag and the flute with me and return them to the sand. People are like grains of sand being thrown about by the wind. Chance brings them together, then they are separated, forever. Buddha said: 'I see the whole vast world in a grain of sand.' Does the Earth still turn on its own axis?

MARY: One day it will stop. It will be tired of bearing all these wars.

AN: [*looking into the distance*] Wars. Yes, wars. All three of us joined the army on the same day. She was a nurse in the Special Intelligence Battalion with us. The War Hero and I, together with another soldier, were selected as the three best scouts. That night, we were ordered to enter the enemy's military compound to uncover their strategic troop movements. We were planning an attack for the next day. [*Looking at the photo*] That night the three of us crawled right up behind the sandbag barrier of the compound and this soldier didn't even see us…

> *The shadows of the two figures in white shrouds can be seen clearly floating into the hut in the world of the dead souls.*

SCENE TWO

A MOMENT OF SILENCE IN THE WAR

Night time in the military compound during the war. The moon is partly hidden by a black cloud, casting a pale light over the sandbag barrier around the compound. In a corner, LAM, AN and PHI, in uniform, carrying guns, snake along the sandbag barrier. Search lights sweep the compound. The air is full of the sound of insects. Suddenly the sound of a flute breaks the silence. LAM, AN and PHI crane their necks towards the sound.

LAM: Damn you! You come here with your guns and bombs to kill innocent people, then have the fucking hide to play music to entertain yourselves at night. [*Cocking his gun*] Let me give that flute-playing fucker a shot in his throat.

AN: [*pushing LAM's gun barrel down*] Don't do it, Lam. If you shoot, you'll give us away. Our orders are to protect the secrecy of tomorrow's attack at all costs.

PHI: [*craning his neck towards the source of the music*] Look at those self-contented, fat bastards smoking cigarettes. The smell is out of this world.

AN: I wonder what those bastards eat to make their skin so white? Shit, this compound is built like a fortress, our unit will need heavy cover fire.

LAM: Just look at that fucking bearded bastard, bolting his food and yapping. Isn't he disgustingly ugly? Human beings are strange. All built the same—with a mouth, a tongue and teeth—but all speak so fucking differently. But everywhere lions' roars are the same.

AN: Ssh…! Lie down! Here comes the patrol!

> *They lie down. The flute plays.*

PHI: [*lifting his head up*] We are safe. Fuck them. My heart's pounding so bloody hard. Hey. You two. Are you afraid of death?

AN: Isn't everyone?

LAM: Not this Lam. I never worry about death.

PHI: If you had one last word, what would it be?

LAM: Kill!

AN: No! Mine would be 'live'. I want to live. This war has made me long to be alive even more. Listen to that flute. It sounds so sad.

PHI: [*in serious voice*] Comrade An! Don't let the music of the enemy distract you from your fighting spirit.

LAM: Fucking fool. Talking about music and poetry in the battlefields as if you're on the fucking moon. If all our soldiers were like you, romantic shit, we would have lost this fucking land a long time ago.

AN: It is almost time for the attack. I have to contact base for cover fire. Follow me now and keep down.

LAM: [*looking to the direction of the flute play*] Fuck you! Go on playing your flute. Go on laughing your head off! Tomorrow I'll show you who the fuck I am.

> LAM, AN *and* PHI, *holding their guns, snake away silently. The flute continues with the same insistent melancholy. The light changes. A long silence. Then suddenly the earth rumbles with noises from heavy artillery and the battle cries of soldiers. Clouds of dirt and sand erupt. The painful cries of wounded soldiers lost in the gunfire can be heard. The sound of approaching aircraft becomes increasingly loud.* LAM, AN *and* PHI *can be seen in three different positions, gritting their teeth and firing away.*

[*Roaring angrily*] Fuck you! I won't let even one single fucker return home alive.

PHI: [*calling out to* LAM] Lam! Be careful! Their planes are coming to their aid.

AN: [*yelling out with great fear*] Watch out! Lam! Run fast! Fire! Fire! The planes are dropping napalm bombs! Run! Lam! Run!

> *The light changes. The battlefield is suddenly covered by fire.* LAM*'s face is caught by the fire. His gun drops and he falls face down.* AN *and* PHI *quickly run over the help him. Only the desperate, painful cries of the soldiers caught by the fire can be heard.*

LAM: [*clutching his face*] An! Phi! My face is burned! Too hot! Too fucking hot!

AN: [*shaking and calling* LAM] Lam! Lam! It is me, it's An!

LAM: [*roaring with pain*] Where are our comrades?

PHI: [*his throat choking with smoke*] All gone. With the fire.

LAM: I am burning hot! Too fucking hot! No, I can't die now, Lam will have to avenge this bloody face! Blood has to pay for blood.

PHI: [*carrying* LAM *over his shoulder*] Stop yelling! Of course you'll live! The Nation and the People are with you! [*To* AN] I'll take Comrade Lam to the river. You go and look for the Unit's nurse. Go and find Mai. Run quickly.

> PHI *takes* LAM *and runs in one direction,* AN, *with his gun, runs in another direction. The gunfire slowly abates. The light changes to reveal a bloody and quiet battlefield. Smoke rises from the burning bodies scattered on the white sand. The air is thick with the smell of gunfire. From the smoke the figures in the white shrouds emerge as if the souls of the dead are returning to the living world.*
>
> *The first figure takes off its shroud revealing himself as a foreign soldier. It is* GABRIEL *in his uniform, writhing with pain. His leg has been badly wounded in the battle. He is trying to crawl away from the charred bodies.*
>
> *The second figure takes off its shroud, revealing itself as a female nurse. It is* MAI, *a beautiful girl carrying her first-aid bag with the sign of the Red Cross, pistol on her hip. She walks briskly among the bodies checking to see if any of her comrades are still alive. She suddenly spots* GABRIEL*'s movement. She runs to him, quickly pulling out her pistol and pointing it at his head.*

GABRIEL: [*raising both his arms up, trembling*] Please don't shoot!

> MAI *does not understand. She pushes her pistol closer against his head.*

[*Bursting out crying*] Please don't kill me! Please let me live! My wife and my little girl are waiting for me.

> MAI *still does not understand a word. She stares at* GABRIEL *with an intense hatred, her pistol firmly pushed against his head.*

[*Shaking with fear at the prospect of being killed*] Please let me play for the last time—then you can shoot me. Do you understand?

> GABRIEL *pulls out his flute and gently brings it to his mouth. A moment of silence, then music emits from the flute—melodically and softly to the rhythm of his painful breathing.* MAI *looks at* GABRIEL, *bewildered, while listening to his playing. Suddenly the playing becomes intermittent and weaker.* MAI, *confused, looks at the cocked pistol in her hand and into* GABRIEL*'s eyes which gaze at hers fixedly.* GABRIEL *puts his finger to his head as if to indicate that he is ready to die. In the deepest, silent moment of war, the pistol slips off* MAI*'s hand. She opens her water bottle and gently drips water into his mouth, then quickly pulls the first-aid kit from her bag and begins to fix up his leg wound.* GABRIEL *is close to death.*
>
> *Dust settles slowly over the dead bodies. The light changes. The sun finally sets in the distance, the desert becoming a vast darkness.* MAI *takes out a piece of parachute cloth and places it over* GABRIEL. *The darkness becomes total.* MAI *makes a fire. In the flickering light of the fire,* GABRIEL *slowly regains consciousness.*

[*Pointing his finger to his temple*] Why didn't you shoot me?

> MAI *does not understand what he is saying. She gently shakes her head.* GABRIEL *takes off his watch, his pendant and ring, giving them to* MAI.

Thank you for not killing me, I'll be grateful to you for the rest of my life. Please take them, I want you to have them.

> MAI *looks at them and shakes her head.*

[*Surprised*] What is your name?

MAI *doesn't understand his words. She takes his flute, looking at it in silence, before handing it back to him.*

GABRIEL *takes the flute from her.*

MAI *looks at him, smiling.*

The sound of the flute breaks the silence of the night. MAI *is lost in the music, which gradually fades away.* MAI *looks at* GABRIEL *and starts singing a familiar song.* GABRIEL *listens to her attentively, then begins to accompany her on the flute.*

Suddenly two torchlight beams appear from the opposite direction, cutting short the music and the singing. LAM *and* PHI, *with guns in their hands, come out from the dark.* LAM'*s head is bandaged with a piece of cloth torn from his uniform, showing only half of his face.* LAM *and* PHI *stare coldly at* MAI *and* GABRIEL. MAI *fearfully looks at the guns pointing at her.*

MAI: I looked for you everywhere. I thought you were all dead! [*Choking with tears*] A lot of our comrades have been burned to death. I don't know who survived and who didn't. I came across this injured soldier who was waiting to die and I helped him.

> PHI *furiously steps forward, pointing his cocked gun at* GABRIEL'*s head.* MAI *knocks* PHI'*s gun upwards and it discharges into the air.*

No! Please don't kill him. [*She shows them the flute.*] He is a musician. He plays beautifully.

> *She hands the flute to* GABRIEL.

Please listen, I have never heard such beautiful music!

> GABRIEL *takes the flute back, looking at* LAM *and* PHI *in fear. Then slowly he brings the flute to his lips.* PHI *suddenly strikes the flute from* GABRIEL'*s hands.* GABRIEL *is trembling like a leaf.*

[*Stunned*] Why? Why won't you listen to the flute?

LAM: [*his cold voice cutting like a knife*] We heard it last night!

MAI: [*frightened, stepping back to avoid* PHI'*s hateful stare*] Why do you look at me with such hatred?

PHI: [*spitting at her face*] You traitor! The Party and the People will never believe that you could spare the life of an enemy who brought death and destruction to this desert and then sing to entertain him.

MAI: [*tearfully*] Please, Lam, I never thought of betraying our country.

LAM: [*coldly*] Never speak my name again.

MAI: [*pleading*] Let me explain. He's badly injured and close to death. I could not bring myself to kill him. His flute sounded like a plea for life. Out of habit I began to sing to myself—not to the enemy. Please believe me. I did not sing for him, I am not a traitor.

LAM: [*without any feeling*] You have the right to sing to anybody, you have the right to save anybody. No one in this poor desert dare to reproach you. [*His voice hardens and he points to the bodies of the soldiers.*] Just take a good look. Who cares about the souls of over three hundred and sixty dead soldiers of our Special Intelligence Battalion? All gone.

MAI: No one else? Even An, was he also killed?

PHI: [*spitting in her face*] He survived. Now he'll never agree to marry you, you traitor.

LAM: [*with no feeling*] Stop reproaching her. She has been a source of joy and she has fought bravely with our Battalion. It is pointless to reproach her. [*Pointing again to the dead soldier*] We'll use the uniforms of the dead solders to tie her up with the enemy she saved and burn them alive as a sacrifice to the souls. The souls of young soldiers who died without being loved. Young soldiers who never had the chance to hear her sweet singing.

> PHI *eagerly goes off to strip the uniforms from the dead soldiers and uses them to tie up* MAI *and* GABRIEL.

PHI: You deserve this. Bastard, invader, and you, you traitor.

MAI: [*on her knees, begging*] Please, I beg you. Please don't. [*Choking with tears, pleading and begging*] Please, Lam! Let me live! I beg you! Please, I beg you. I am not a traitor! I am your friend. Please, for the sake of our friendship, forgive me. Let me live!

LAM: Friendship has been destroyed by fire. And fire is repaid with fire! Blood is repaid with blood. Death with death. My heart now beats for victory. Burn them.

> PHI *starts the fire.* MAI *and* GABRIEL *are burned alive. The painful cries of the victims burst out as the flames leap into the air. Slowly the fire dies out. Only smoke rises up from the charred skeletons.* PHI *and* LAM *stand in silence looking at the remains. After a while* AN, *with his gun slung from his shoulder, comes in, his face blackened. He carries a bag laden with things he has collected from the dead solders. Exhausted, he falls on his knees.*

AN: I can't recognise anybody! Fire has turned our entire Battalion into charred meat. Only the three of us survived. I heard the gunfire and saw the fire burning. I guessed it must be you! Did you find Mai?

> LAM *coldly points to the rising curls of the smoke.* AN *rushes to the ashes and the skeletal remains. He picks up the first-aid bag.*

Even Mai?

> *Without any emotion,* LAM *stares at the pile of ashes and nods his head.* PHI *clicks his heels and stands to attention.*

PHI: [*seriously declaring*] We burned alive the traitor and the invader as a sacrifice for our dead comrades.

AN: [*stupefied*] Burned alive? Traitor? What? What are you saying?

> PHI *clicks his heels again, standing to attention.*

PHI: [*seriously declaring loudly*] I said: We burned alive the traitor and the invader as a sacrifice for our dead comrades!

AN: Who burned her?

> *Coldly and without emotion,* LAM *points to himself.*

Why?

PHI: She was caught helping an enemy and singing to entertain him as well!

> AN *runs over to* LAM *and shakes his shoulders.*

AN: Is that true? Did you burn her alive?

> LAM *coldly nods his head.*

Did you know I loved her?

> LAM *coldly nods his head again*

PHI: [*clicking his heels, in a loud voice*] The Party and the People will find you another wife. The Party and the People would never allow you to marry a traitor! Be strong in trying times! We will win! The enemy will have to lose. Have faith in our ideal which we are pursuing. The Party and the People will never leave you without a wife!

AN: [*shocked*] Singing doesn't make her a traitor!

PHI: [*clicking his heels, in all seriousness*] Singing to enemies in any way means having intentions to betray the great revolutionary achievements of the People.

AN: [*furiously angry*] Have you forgotten?! The order is to not maltreat any prisoners of war! Even if she was really guilty of betrayal, she would have had to be tried by the military court! Why did you burn them alive? Who gave you that right?

LAM: [*roaring like a wounded beast, pointing to his bandaged half-face*] This is the military court! This half-burned military court gave that order!

> AN *swiftly points his gun at* LAM. PHI, *as swiftly, points his gun at* AN. *They stare at each other for a time and in silence.* LAM *signals to* PHI *to put his gun down. He walks slowly, opening his shirt to expose his chest to* AN.

[*In a low and slow voice*] Shoot me! Go on, shoot me! [*Suddenly he roars like a wounded lion.*] Go on, shoot me! You think I am afraid of death! Go on, shoot me!

> AN, *trembling, drops his gun. He takes short, slow steps toward the smouldering ashes, before slumping slowly to the ground, holding his head and crying uncontrollably.*

[*Following* AN, *his voice again without emotion*] Why are you crying? Never cry.

> *He puts the gun barrel in* AN*'s mouth.*

[*Yelling*] I forbid you! Tears cannot save the White Sand Desert. Sit up! Compose a poem, so the next generation can remember that here lay over three hundred and sixty young, loveless soldiers, all burned to death on the same day!

> LAM *exits quickly and firmly.*

PHI: [*clicking his heels, standing to attention, repeating* LAM*'s words in a dry voice*] Tears cannot save the White Sand Desert. Comrade An! Be strong in these trying times. The Party and the People believe in you. Sit up! Compose a poem!

> PHI *exits quickly. Under the pale and soft light of the half-hidden moon,* AN *crawls around the smouldering ashes. He spots the damaged flute, picks it up and puts it in the first-aid bag. In silence,* AN *looks up to the moon. The* VOICE *of someone reciting a poem comes from somewhere in the distance of the desert at night.*

VOICE: The meat party is over
only one faithful lover is left
sitting here
amongst white bones and charred bodies

chanting for the souls of the dead to return
the young girl has gone never to sing again
oh war…!
why did you rob and take away
young men and girls
of my homeland
of the mothers over there, across the ocean, who cry silently
under the heavy afternoon sky with shadows of flying crows
the meat party is over
one is still sitting here
waiting for the other to reappear out of the white sand dunes
out of the moon in the lover's heart!

The shadows of the two figures in white shrouds move gently in the distance.

SCENE THREE

THE LAST LANDMINE EXPLOSION IN THE WHITE SAND DESERT

The scene is the same as for Act One Scene One. LAM *is still in his well-pressed suit, bedecked with medals. He is standing in silence next to the tank. His face is haggard and more aged. He slowly feels the sand-covered caterpillar-track of the tank with his hand. The eerie cries of crows are heard in the distance.* QUAN *runs in, worried.*

QUAN: Father. Why are you here?

LAM: I am paying a visit to the past.

QUAN: Yes, Father. If it pleases you, I will tell the workers to build a wall around this tank and have your name inscribed to remind the People of your glorious achievements!

LAM: I hope people remember my deeds. They shouldn't need an inscription.

QUAN: Excuse me, Father. What is bothering you? I heard you toss and turn all night.

LAM: I think you should get yourself a career!

QUAN: [*surprised*] But, Father, I'm the Chairman of the Local Council—

LAM: You're stupid.

QUAN: I'm sorry, Father. Why do you say that?

LAM: One day, the Communists will lose their power in the White Sand Desert. Then what are you going to do? Return to the fields and be a slave like your ancestors?

QUAN: No, Father. Nothing can destroy our great achievements in the White Sand Desert.

LAM: [*becoming angry*] Always—'Yes, Father', 'No, Father', 'Excuse me, Father'—that doesn't get you anywhere. You stupid fool.

   A long intense silence.

Tell me, where the Communist power has collapsed, are the Communists being executed? Has anybody been hanged? Has anybody been beheaded by a hoe? Has anybody been drowned in soapy water?

QUAN: No, Father. I don't know.

LAM: You don't know! What is the point in being a leader then?

QUAN: Please, Father! The world has changed a great deal.

LAM: [*dumbfounded*] And you have kept me in the dark! What right do you have?

QUAN: I just didn't want you to spend the rest of your life feeling disappointed.

LAM: How could things collapse so fast?

QUAN: You sit at home all day, admiring your medals, dreaming about Socialism, oblivious to the fact that people no longer think like you. If I had just closed my eyes and followed you, our people would have died from starvation long ago.

LAM: Do people still remember my name?

QUAN: I will always remember you, you are my father and I love you.

LAM: Do you really love me?

QUAN: Yes, I do. And I respect you.

LAM: Whatever happens to me, will you still love and respect me as you say?

QUAN: You are a fine example for me to follow. Whatever happens, I shall always love and respect you.

LAM: Say whatever you want to say, do whatever you want to do. But make sure that your father is not going to be left in the sun to die!

QUAN: Why do you say that?

LAM: Anything might happen. People change. Politics change.

QUAN: Do you mean the stories the crazy old man told me are true?

LAM: What if they are and what if they are not?

QUAN: [*embarrassed*] If the old man's stories were true, then…

LAM: … then would you kill me? You just said you would love and respect me for the rest of your life!

QUAN: Yes, Father. But now only you and I are here. Please tell me, are his stories true?

A silent moment.

LAM: Go! Leave me. Stop asking stupid questions. I have never been afraid of death.

QUAN: What do you mean?

LAM: Just go!

QUAN: Where can I go now? Please let me stay with you.

LAM: I go my own way. Our roads lead in opposite directions.

QUAN: Where does your road lead? And where does mine?

LAM: I go back to the past with all the things that people want to forget. You go to the future and you must do things that people will want to remember. Go now! Quickly, before I become angry.

QUAN: [*afraid*] I am going. [*Intending to go*] Goodbye, Father!

LAM: Quan! My son!

QUAN: [*turning*] Yes, Father?

LAM: Come here. I want to shake your hand!

He shakes QUAN*'s hand.*

In future, if anyone asks you where is the person who burned this tank, please tell them that he has gone into oblivion. Now go!

QUAN: [*tearfully*] Father…

LAM: [*gravely*] Go! Never cry. Tears cannot save this White Sand Desert.

QUAN *exits quickly.* LAM *watches his shadow disappear, then holds his head, before bursting out crying like a baby. He bangs his head against the side of the tank. The* CRONE *comes in, carrying the dirty, heavy bag on her back.*

The Crone!

The CRONE *empties out skulls and bones from the bag and sits down. She proceeds to clean them with her shirt front.*

CRONE: Where do you come from? How do you know my name?

LAM: [*whispering*] From Hell!

CRONE: Is it a happy place down there?

LAM: For some it is, for others it is a sad place! Did you find those bones in the compound?

CRONE: Why do you ask? Do you know anyone among them?

LAM: I knew them all.

CRONE: Isn't that enough? Why come here again? Aren't you scared of death?

LAM: [*with a grave face*] No. This Lam is never afraid of death.

CRONE: Once upon a time, there were long-legged creatures who brought along a rain of fire to pour over the short-legged creatures. [*Singing*] 'La… la… la…' Do you want to find the long or the short bones?

LAM: I want to find my own. [*Whispering*] I have just begun looking for them. I don't know if I will find them.

CRONE: The more you look, the harder they are to find. Don't look for it and you'll find it. The world is blind, no one sees anything. Now go away! I have to prepare breakfast for my children.

> LAM *crawls away toward the compound. The* CRONE *takes the bones and climbs onto the tank to enter the compartment.* AN *and* MARY *enter. Silently, they sit on the exposed roots of the tree.* AN *respectfully lights some incense sticks, planting them in the sand next to the tree roots. The shadows of the two figures in white shrouds move gently amongst the incense smoke.*

AN: Each time I light the incense and pray for their souls, I have the feeling that they are still living here.

MARY: [*choking with emotion*] Did you plant this tree?

AN: Yes. I buried the remains of your father and Mai here. I planted the tree over their grave. For years, the tree grew very quickly.

MARY: Can you take me to the soldier who carried out the orders? Who burned alive my father and Mai. I just want to see his face.

AN: [*sadly*] He died a while ago. When I heard that he was gravely ill, I went to visit him. It was he who told me the whole story. He died full of remorse with his eyes open. Not many attended his funeral, just armies of ants. I remember clearly that I accidentally stepped on the leader ant and all the soldier ants were in disarray, crawling around the dead leader in the middle of my footprint.

Silence.

MARY: That footprint seems to have a soul.

AN: Everybody asked why he was not buried in the war heroes' cemetery of this desert, but he said, in his will, he wished to be buried like an ordinary person.

MARY: Have you seen the War Hero who burned this tank again?

AN: No. I haven't. But I hear he is known everywhere for his victorious battles!

MARY: Why don't you find another lover to console you?

AN: [*looking far away into the sand dunes*] Here, in this desert, there is a bird that lives with one partner all its life. If one dies, the other stays faithful until its own death. All my life, I've only loved Mai. And I've dreamt of becoming a poet like your father dreamt of becoming a flautist.

MARY: And neither of you realised your dreams.

A long silence.

AN: [*suddenly pointing to the sky*] Look. Do you see the red over there? It looks exactly like the kite my old friend used to make when we were young!

MARY: It's the same as the one your old friend gave me.

AN: That's right! He loved the colour red!

MARY: Which colour do you like?

AN: I also like red. But my red is that of the sun.

MARY: And his red?

AN: Perhaps of blood!

MARY: But red is red!

AN: No, there are differences.

MARY: When you die, do you want to go to Hell or Heaven?

AN: [*after thinking*] I want to go to Hell!

MARY: Why?

AN: If I don't go to Hell, how can I find the old friend who made those wonderful kites for me?!

A long silence.

MARY: You two are alike, yet so different. [*Pause.*] I am going this evening. It is probably the last time I'll see you.

AN: Aren't you coming back to collect the remains of your father?

MARY: Dig up this tree? No!

AN: It is the only way to get your father's remains. I carefully put his and Mai's ashes in a cannon shell and buried them under the tree!

MARY: [*moved*] This is my father's second home. Please leave his soul and his bones to be forever with those of Mai beneath this tree. Let them remind us of our hope for the good and beautiful things of life that will never be lost!

> *A landmine explodes loudly in the compound area. The* CRONE *appears on top of the tank, holding pieces of Lam's clothing. She looks sorrowfully toward the compound.*

AN: [*puzzled, asking the* CRONE] Who gave you those pieces of clothing?

MARY: Whose are they?

CRONE: The one who wants to go and look for his own bones!

MARY: Who?

CRONE: [*pointing to the compound where the landmine exploded*] He went to where all the souls of the dead come from.

> AN *runs out quickly.*

MARY: [*calling out*] Mr An! Where are you going?

AN: I am looking for my friend, the beautiful kite-maker.

CRONE: [*standing on top of the tank like a statue*] Don't leave me here alone.

MARY: [*climbing onto the top of the tank, standing next to the* CRONE] Crone! Crone. I am staying here. With you.

> *Landmines continue to explode from the distant compound. The* CRONE *holds on to* MARY *and cries.* MARY *takes the* CRONE *in her arms. The dead souls in white shrouds appear. Their voices become audible as the explosions diminish and fade away.*

FIRST SOUL: Perhaps it was because of his music. The flute prevented me from raising my gun. Please do not think because I am sand that I can become a traitor!

SECOND SOUL: Please, don't shoot me. Let me live. My wife and my little girl.

THIRD SOUL: Sit up and compose a good poem to remind people that here lay over three hundred and sixty young, unloved soldiers, who were burned to death on the same day.

FOURTH SOUL: He is still alive, but he will never marry a traitor like you!

FIFTH SOUL: Outside the storm is abating. Do you hear the wind caressing the sand dunes? Let the children free to fly kites, to play and to sing on the dunes of this White Sand Desert!

> QUAN *enters. He looks toward the now silent compound in the distance. He then briskly walks toward the tree with the old, bleached, wooden sign in the shape of an arrow nailed on its trunk, with the written warning: 'Danger! Landmines! Keep Out!'*

QUAN: [*calling to* MARY] Excuse me, Mary. Please help me take this sign down.

MARY: [*climbing down from the tank*] Why?

QUAN: Those are the last landmine explosions in the White Sand Desert.

> *His mobile phone rings and he starts to hunt around for it in the sand.*

CRONE: [*standing on top of the tank, singing at the top of her voice*]
The storm is over
my children, come and eat!
This rice comes from the dried fields of our land.
This fish comes from the dried rivers of our land.
My love for you is like the sunshine over these vast sand dunes.
Please eat, my children,
then I will tell you a story:
Once upon a time there lived a young man and a young girl…

> *In the distance, the birds are singing, welcoming a new day. The light fades slowly with the singing of the* CRONE.

THE END

A Graveyard for the Living

Translated by Lien Yeomans

Translation edited by May-Brit Akerholt

CHARACTERS

MRS DAT, an old woman who lives by herself in a thatched hut on a river peninsula somewhere in the Red River Delta in Northern Vietnam, aged 66

CON, Mrs Dat's son, Chairman of the City Management Committee, aged 45

MR THÉ, childhood friend of Mrs Dat, Con's supervisor, aged 66

OLD SON, an old eccentric who shares the peninsula with Mrs Dat, aged 66

LIEN, Con's wife, aged 35

HANG, Con and Lien's daughter, student of Fine Arts, aged 16

During the Land Reform Movement in 1954 in North Vietnam, thousands of innocent people suffered injustice, unnecessary pain and misery, and untimely death. In writing this play, the writer prays that those who suffered these atrocities will be reborn into a world where ignorance and lies are not allowed to repeat this tragedy.

All characters and events in this play are fictitious. The story happens on a river bank of a peninsula somewhere in the Red River Delta in North Vietnam toward the end of the last decade of the twentieth century, during the period of reconstruction and revaluation of past mistakes in New Vietnam.

PART ONE

SCENE ONE

THE SUN AND THE FAST FLOWING RIVER

A peninsula of land jutting into a fast flowing river. It's sunset. The glowing red sun looks like an eye filled with fire that pierces the clouds. Behind a row of green trees, boats are bobbing up and down on the river.

OLD SON *sleeps in front of a thatched hut, curled up on the ground next to a garden bed. His body, naked except for a loin cloth, acts as a fence to protect the young seedlings in the garden. Inside the hut,* MRS DAT *sits silently facing the altar where incense is burning. She wears an old, faded, brown habit and a scarf covering her head.* HANG *sits on the riverbank drawing the sunset. The boatmen's sad song can be heard.* OLD SON *is having a nightmare.*

OLD SON: [*beating the ground with his hands*] You bastard! Why don't you answer me when I call. Get up! Get up! I'm going to sing you a song, you hear?

HANG: Go back to sleep. You're raving. Who are you talking to anyway?

OLD SON: My old friend from jail.

HANG: Why on Earth do you call your friend a bastard?

OLD SON: I called and called and he didn't answer. I thought it was because he hated me. But of course he's been dead for a long time. Those animals killed him with a chopstick. They pushed it in one ear till it came out through the other, so no one should know they'd murdered him.

    He looks at the chopstick in his hand.

HANG: Stop it, you're making my flesh crawl.

OLD SON: If you don't believe me, come and touch his body. It's as cold as a piece of frozen meat.

HANG: [*frightened*] Every time I see you, you dream about nothing but death.

OLD SON: It's all true, as sure as one and one are two. Don't you dare tell me it's a dream.

HANG: Let's talk about something else.

OLD SON: Yesterday we found a huge dead rat in the gaol's water tank. The prisoners are begging for the tank to be cleaned. But the gaoler screams at them: 'This is a prison, not a piece of paradise!'

HANG: You're just making it up. When were you in gaol?

OLD SON: If you want to know when, Hang, go and ask history.

> *He laughs insanely and sings, keeping time like a conductor with the chopstick.*

[*Singing*] 'Spiders spinning webs, bees looking for honey, silk worms making cocoons, dogs guarding houses and humans killing each other.' Ha, ha, ha, ha. [*Counting his seedlings as he sings*] 'One body has two legs, two arms, two eyes, one trunk and one head. Two bodies have four legs, four arms, four eyes, two trunks and two heads. Three bodies have six legs, six—'

HANG: Please, Old Son, I want to finish my drawing.

OLD SON: [*dancing over to* HANG, *laughing crazily*] Drawing the sun again? Even the bright sun cannot chase away the darkness of the night. All the rivers empty their water into the sea, yet the sea is never full. Forget about drawing them, they're abstract concepts.

HANG: So what else do you want me to draw?

OLD SON: [*pointing to the ground as if he can see another life through it*] There you are. See if you can draw what's going on down there. [*He laughs crazily.*] Quick, draw this. A group of people are being pushed through the gates of Hell.

> *He pulls* HANG *to him, beating his hands on the ground.* HANG *is trembling with fear.*

There, can you see it? They're being tortured. They chop off the boy's hands, they poke out the girl's eyes and slice off the woman's ears. Blood is pouring out everywhere. And look, now they cut off the old man's head. He won't have a place to put his hat now. Quick, quick, quick, draw them! Draw them before they all disappear!

HANG: Let me go!

OLD SON: [*screaming at the ground*] Hey! Hey, you down there! You're going to Hell, and yet you're laughing. Draw him. Draw that man who's laughing.

HANG: [*running to the hut, angrily looking back at* OLD SON] Silly old fool!

OLD SON: [*laughing crazily*] They're pushing and shoving each other into the muddy ground. No, no, it is not me! My family owns no buffalos, no cows, no fields, no orchards. [*He falls over, his mouth foaming.*] It isn't me. Please, don't mutilate me. Help me! Help me.

> *He passes out in his hallucination.* MRS DAT *sits silently like a statue.*

HANG: Grandma, Old Son's carrying on like a lunatic. One minute he's sleeping peacefully [like a baby], the next he's raving and screaming, I can't stand it…

MRS DAT: Perhaps he is angry with someone sneaking off with his dreams. Don't listen to his stories.

HANG: But are the stories true, grandma?

MRS DAT: [*indifferent*] Pay no attention to the dreams of a madman. [*Pause.*] When is your father coming to take you back to the city?

HANG: Soon. I don't really want to go back. I want to stay here with you.

MRS DAT: You are going back. You have to study. It's enough for me that you visit now and then.

> *Pause.*

HANG: I love you. I want to paint your portrait.

MRS DAT: [*sitting down facing the wall, immobile*] Please, Hang, don't even think about it. Young people ought to look for something fresh and interesting. Here, all you'll find is old mad Son and me, and our fast flowing river.

HANG: Did you have long hair when you were young? Why did you shave your hair off?

MRS DAT: It was very, very long, my dear. A young man looked at me and sang: 'The sun shines as bright as your lips. The rain is as sad as your eyes. Every strand of your hair floats like ocean waves.'

HANG: What a sad song.

> *Pause.*

MRS DAT: How are your parents these days?

HANG: They're in the middle of a cold war. I don't like my parents very much.

MRS DAT: Children should love their parents.

HANG: Mum and Dad don't care about you, do they? Whenever I mention you, they change the topic. I knew you weren't well, but I had to beg my father before he'd let me come and see you. You should go to the hospital for some rest. I'll pay for it. I just sold some of my paintings. I can afford it, you know.

MRS DAT: Thank you for your kind thoughts. But all I need is to stay here and pray.

HANG: What do you pray for every day?

MRS DAT: I pray that the beautiful things in life will not be lost. I pray for a bright future for my granddaughter.

> OLD SON *suddenly sits up and beats both hands on the ground, screaming at the top of his voice to sounds from the dead souls coming from deep inside the earth.*

OLD SON: You bastards! You talk too much. Don't you know it only takes three years to learn to speak but seventy years to learn to be silent? You're living in Hell but you don't realise it!

> *The songs from the dead souls suddenly stop.* OLD SON *starts counting the trees.*

One body has two legs…

MRS DAT: Sorrow has returned to this peninsula. I haven't slept well the last few days. Old Son's been screaming every night. The souls of the untimely dead are demanding their lives back through his mouth.

HANG: Grandma, why does Old Son keep counting the trees?

MRS DAT: He planted the trees along the river and gave each tree a name. Each of those names reminds him of a life.

OLD SON: Hey, you down there! [*Singing*] 'Don't be human in your next existence. Be a tree out in the open and sing with the wind.'

MRS DAT: He was a very handsome and clever young man once.

OLD SON: [*resuming his conversation with the invisible people*] Do you want me to go fishing with you? Oh no, I've been hooked once in my life, that's enough. What? Am I a writer? No, never. Hey, I'll tell you something—once bitten, twice shy! Don't try to trap me again. I've only got one life. Don't come near me, I don't wish to see you. Stop!

OLD SON *looks around, frightened by the echoes of screams of pain. A mist slowly spreads out, covering the landscape. Through the mist appear mutilated dead souls, some without heads, without arms, without ears, with blood streaming down. They surround* OLD SON *who covers his head with both hands and rolls around on the ground.*

MRS DAT: Don't look at him and don't come here again. All I ask is that you throw some earth into my grave when I die.

HANG: You'll never die, grandma.

MRS DAT: No one can escape death.

HANG: When does a person really die?

MRS DAT: When the heart stops beating.

HANG: I'll be your heart, I'll beat forever so you'll never die. Please come and live with me in the city. I'll make a veil for your face. Please?

MRS DAT: No, I can't. I have to look after Old Son and this peninsula.

HANG: Why do you have to look after him?

MRS DAT: He is my very old friend. We have been friends for a long, long time.

HANG: Why don't you build a proper house? As long as I can remember you've been sitting in this old hut. This isolated place has nothing, it's just an empty space. Why do you have to look after it?

MRS DAT: It has a lot, my dear.

HANG: Is this peninsula man-made, grandma?

MRS DAT: Yes.

HANG: Why did they build it on this river?

MRS DAT: It doesn't matter now. There's no point in knowing their purpose. Knowing why doesn't change anything. Ah, there's your father.

CON *enters, suitably dressed for a high-ranking officer. He looks indifferently at* OLD SON *who is rolling on the ground. All of a sudden, he gives the old man a kick which brings him out of his nightmare.*

A long silence.

CON *stares at the old man without any emotion.* HANG *looks at her father anxiously.* OLD SON *looks at* CON *with an inane smile. When he sees* CON*'s cold, steely eyes, he stands up and walks away.*

CON: I'm surprised to see that lunatic's still around. I thought he died a long time ago.

MRS DAT: He is only alive as a breathing piece of flesh.

CON: Hang, wait for me in the car, I need to talk to Grandma.

> HANG *doesn't move.*

Hurry, please.

HANG: [*looking at* CON, *frightened*] Grandma, I have to go. I'll leave you this painting, I've called it 'The Sun and the Fast Flowing River'. I love you, Grandma. Goodbye.

MRS DAT: Goodbye, my dear granddaughter, I'll pray for you.

> HANG *leaves, looking at* CON *out of the corner of her eye.* CON *stands stiffly. Only his head moves.*
>
> *A long silence.*
>
> CON *stares at* MRS DAT.

I'm nearly seventy years old now. I only have a short time left in this world. I beg you to leave me in peace.

CON: I only have one question. And you will answer me with the truth.

MRS DAT: You mustn't ask me questions I can't answer. Your father died a long time ago. He died before you were born.

CON: I'm not here to ask about my father. I've dealt with those who kept taunting me for being the bastard of the scar-faced woman.

MRS DAT: I never taught you to kill people. I cursed the night you were conccived, but I still love you. All mothers love their children.

CON: I'm not here to ask for your maternal love. I've received orders from my superiors to prepare this area for a new construction—a development of luxury flats for the Party officials.

MRS DAT: It's more useful to feed the hungry, to repair the dyke for the next flood, build schools for the children and care for the old.

CON: It's an order, that's all I know. Please prepare to leave, Mother.

MRS DAT: I would like to stay and take care of all the dispossessed souls.

CON: Life ends with death. There's nothing left to take care of.

MRS DAT: Only bodies die. Souls live forever.

CON: How many people are buried here on this peninsula?

> *Tears stop* MRS DAT *from speaking.*
>
> *A long silence.*

I asked you a question. Why don't you answer me. [*Shouting loudly*] Come on, answer me! Now!

MRS DAT: [*trembling with fear*] Many… many of them… my son.

CON: How many is many? One hundred, two hundred, one thousand, two thousand?

> MRS DAT *sobs.*

[*Screaming*] How many?

MRS DAT: [*trembling, her hands folded over her chest*] I beg you, don't shout at me. Every time you shout, my heart sinks.

CON: Why does your heart sink?

> *Silence.*

When I ask a question, I want an answer. How many?

MRS DAT: My dear son… please… don't…

> *The earth suddenly moves violently. Voices rise from the ground.* MRS DAT *beats the wooden fish irregularly with trembling hands.* CON *walks around mumbling as if he is counting the bodies buried underneath.* OLD SON *waves his chopstick while he dances and sings among the trees on the river bank.*

OLD SON: [*singing*] 'One body has two legs, two arms, two eyes, one trunk, and one head. Two bodies have four legs, four arms, four eyes, two trunks, and two heads. Three bodies have six legs, six arms, six eyes, three trunks, and three heads. Four bodies have eight legs, eight arms, eight eyes, four trunks, and four heads. Fifty bodies have one hundred legs…'

> OLD SON *continues to sing loudly.* CON *is absorbed in his counting. The sun becomes redder, like an angry eye filled with fire. The light fades slowly to the beating of the wooden fish and the singing. The lights go out.*

SCENE TWO

THE DIFFERENT WINDS OF TIME

It is evening. We are in Con and Lien's stylish dining room. In the middle of the room is a large table covered completely by a red tablecloth. The room is filled with smoke from incense and lit with flickering candles.

CON *sits opposite* MR THÉ *in tense silence. The food on the table remains untouched.* MR THÉ *chain smokes.* CON *bends over his drink.*

A long silence.

MR THÉ *places a small pistol on the table.*

MR THÉ: A little present for you, a memento from the war. This pistol has been with me all my life. I offer it to you because I love you as if you were my own son.

CON: I'm grateful for your affection. [*Examining the pistol carefully*] It's still loaded.

MR THÉ: There's only one bullet left. I was about to shoot the last bullet into the air when we'd won the war. But I changed my mind. A gun without a bullet is like a person without a soul.

CON: Your generation gave up everything to fight for our independence and freedom. We will never forget your achievement.

MR THÉ: Are you sure no one can hear our conversation?

CON: My wife and daughter won't be back till late. Please, have some food while it's still hot.

MR THÉ: I'm not interested in food. I'm more interested in your report. How are you progressing with the new construction?

CON: The City Management Committee is running into a lot of problems.

MR THÉ: Please don't play games. I know you're not serious about this project because I haven't decided how to divide the profits.

CON: No, that's not true. I wouldn't dare.

MR THÉ: What percentage do you want? What do you think your reward should be?

CON: I'll accept whatever you decide to give me.

MR THÉ: I'll give you a promotion to whatever position you want to have in the Committee.

CON: I'm not really interested in a promotion.

MR THÉ: What would you think if I appointed someone else to head this project?

CON: I trust you wouldn't write me off.

MR THÉ: You've changed.

CON: You don't like me anymore.

MR THÉ: Times change, so do people. I don't like the way you behave these days. We could be discarded if we don't learn to bend with the winds of change…

CON *remains politely silent.*

Oh, please, don't pretend to be good or ignorant. Every time you've eliminated someone, I've covered for you.

CON: I shall be indebted to you all my life. I apologise if I've disappointed you.

MR THÉ: The Party officials demand that we build houses for them on that land. They love the view.

CON: But the surveyors report to me that there are many human remains under that land.

MR THÉ: [I know that.] That's why we have to find a secret way to destroy all those remains. The wives [of powerful members] don't want the bones of the dead bodies underneath their luxury houses.

CON: I really don't know how or where to destroy the human bones. Can you please tell me who the dead people were? I was very surprised when the surveyors reported to me that the land is a mass grave, sir.

MR THÉ: Don't worry about that. Your generation needs to move towards the future, rather than look back on a black page of history. They pay the money, and we do exactly what they want.

CON: I'm also concerned about the reaction of the people living in this region. Do they know that they're living on a mass grave?

MR THÉ: The noisier the publicity, the less people will know what we are doing.

CON: You can trust me on that.

MR THÉ: I don't want to hear empty words, I'd rather see action.

CON: I plan to build a temporary wall surrounding the entire peninsula while the project's in progress. The trucks will deliver building materials during the day and leave at night with the skeletons. The labourers are unemployed youths, with no family, who've come to the city looking for jobs.

MR THÉ: Sounds like a good plan. Yes, it should work. I'll go and have a look at the site. I guess your mother and that old fool are still on the peninsula?

CON: Yes, they are.

MR THÉ: Do you think they'll give us any problems?

CON: Don't worry about them.

MR THÉ: If this plan's exposed… Well, I'll be going.

> *He stands up quickly and walks towards the door.* CON *stands up to follow him.*

CON: Is something wrong?

MR THÉ: My foot's starting to hurt.

CON: I'll see you to the car.

> MR THÉ *and* CON *leave quickly. The empty room looks ghostly with the flickering light.* LIEN, CON's *wife, crawls out from underneath the dining table: a beautiful and sharp-looking woman. She stands next to the table, unruffled.* CON *returns and stares at* LIEN *with cold eyes.*
>
> *A long silence.*

I knew you were down there listening. I could feel your breath.

LIEN: I kept staring at his toeless foot. It was very hard to control myself from laughing.

CON: Why didn't you?

LIEN: Why didn't you pull me out from under the table?

CON: That old fox will eliminate both you and me if he ever finds out [that you know about his scheme].

LIEN: I'm disgusted by what I heard.

CON: I'm waiting for the price of your silence. I know it's going to be expensive. You've been waiting for years for the chance to get a divorce.

> HANG *appears. She hides behind the door, listening.*

LIEN: So do I have your agreement this time?

CON: So that is what you want in exchange.

LIEN: You know I feel nothing for you. I'll swear that I know nothing if you give me a divorce.

CON: My money and my power has never been enough for you.

LIEN: You've acquired your wealth in the most disgusting ways.

CON: [*hissing through his teeth*] If you want to live, you'd better shut your mouth immediately.

LIEN: I know you're scared. You're terrified behind that mask of power. I felt it every time we made love. When you're anxious, your whole body becomes like jelly, unfeeling, cold. That's the sad truth. You're nothing but a cowardly bastard who slaves for the authorities to save your own skin.

CON: There's something I've never told you. All my life I've been trying to find out about my father.

LIEN: Not for my sake, I hope. Even if you came from aristocratic stock, it wouldn't make any difference to me. I only want an ordinary life.

CON: And yet you were so happy when you agreed to marry me.

LIEN: I was a naïve eighteen-year-old girl. How could I have known that the polished appearance of the young politician who'd just returned from overseas was hiding a rotten core? [*Pause.*] I want to find my own life instead of living the lives of people you've destroyed. I want to find the simplicity I've lost living with you.

CON: You know how much I love you.

LIEN: How can you shout at the top of your voice about classless struggle, only to turn around and oppress those classless comrades from your own position of power?

CON: I sacrificed almost everything for you. Don't you remember how happy we were, making love? How you used to cry afterwards?

LIEN: Happy, making love to you? Rape is more like it. I cried because I felt humiliated, not because I was happy. To truly live is to keep searching, learning. Please, Con, let me go.

> *A long silence.*

CON: What about our daughter?

LIEN: She'll be fine. She's finding her own life.

> *A long silence.*

CON: So you want a divorce at any price? [*Pause.*] I agree… but you have to help me one more time.

LIEN: I'll do whatever I can, as long as I can have my divorce.

CON: [*coldly*] You must seduce Thé. He's holding out on me, and I want to know why.

LIEN: You're forcing me to prostitute myself?

CON: I'm not interested in his paltry offers. I need your help to trap him.

LIEN: I can't bear to think I've shared my life with a devious bastard like you.

CON: [*examining the pistol in his hand*] You must realise that the old fox intends to save the last bullet for me if I don't obey him.

LIEN: What will you do to me if I don't agree?

CON: Don't ask me questions you already know the answer to!

LIEN: What is it you need to know from him?

CON: I want to know how much it's worth.

> *He leaves.*

LIEN: All I want is a normal life. Con, I'll find my own way to get it.

> HANG *runs past the doorway.* LIEN *remains alone on the stage. She stares into empty space. The lights fade to black.*

SCENE THREE

THE PAST: A DISAPPOINTED DREAM

Night time on the peninsula. The moon is half hidden behind a dark cloud. Sounds of the wind and the water can be heard in the background. The lights from the ferryboats on the river flicker on and off. Echoes of the boatmen's songs float in the air.

MRS DAT sits still in front of the water. LIEN *sits next to her. She looks into the darkness with anxiety.*

LIEN: This may be the last time I can visit you. Whatever happens, you will always be my mother-in-law.

MRS DAT: Thank you for coming. I know you haven't had much happiness in your life. Follow your heart now. Don't worry about Hang. I'll look after her as long as I live.

LIEN: I haven't seen her for the last few days. How is she?

MRS DAT: She is fine. She follows Old Son around all day, they're tending to the trees. He's much more cheerful now that she's here. You just missed them, they've gone to see the new seedlings on the riverbank.

LIEN: She is so used to luxury. I wonder how she copes with the primitive conditions here?

MRS DAT: I know, I've told her to go home, but she won't listen. She's afraid of her father. And now she's afraid to stay on the peninsula as well. Poor girl! Where can she escape to? She fears both the dead and the living.

LIEN: I'm going away. Perhaps I'll never see you again.

MRS DAT: I know how unhappy you are. I only wish you hadn't married my son.

LIEN: Even my family opposed the marriage. They didn't believe in the ideology Con had devoted his life to. So they disowned me. I had to put all my faith in your son, but it turned out to be an illusion.

MRS DAT: No mother would wish for such a son!

LIEN: It is getting dark so quickly. Looking into this darkness I can't help comparing it with the uncertainty of my life.

MRS DAT: Don't look at the dark night. Come closer. Tomorrow the sun will rise again, and chase away any trace of darkness.

LIEN: I have to go and see Con's boss.

MRS DAT: Why?

LIEN: I've made a deal with your son.

MRS DAT: I feel something bad will happen to you!

LIEN: I have no choice.

MRS DAT: It's hard to be a woman in this land. I love and understand you as if you were my own daughter, but I can't help you.

LIEN: I'll try and make the best of what I have left of my life. I'm sorry we couldn't make our marriage work. I may not visit you very often, but you are always in my thoughts. You are a good mother despite your son.

MRS DAT: My son will be cursed if he digs up bones for greed. Lord Buddha, if only I had died with everybody else, I wouldn't have given birth to this son of mine.

She is choking with tears.

LIEN: Those who were buried here… how did they die?

MRS DAT: It's pointless to talk about old sad stories.

LIEN: Don't hide it from me. I know we're sitting on top of a giant common grave. Please, tell me about it… You're crying… is your life nothing but tears?

MRS DAT: My tears will be transformed into rain drops, into waterfalls, into singing brooks and huge rivers which all flow into the sea. Old Son sings that all the rivers flow into the sea, and yet the sea is never full.

LIEN: I know you've been suffering in silence.

MRS DAT: I don't mind suffering for myself. I only hope you will forgive me for my son who brought you so much unhappiness.

LIEN: I'm not here to accuse you. I need you to tell me about those who were buried here.

The earth rumbles as if thousands of skeletons are moving. Loud noises and painful screaming. The sounds of crows crying from the dark space outside.

MRS DAT: This peninsula was once just a riverbank. They had to mine it with explosives to dig large graves for those who were killed after the war. Slowly it became a peninsula. The river flows along, carrying all the sad memories, and leaving behind the silt to protect the bones of the deceased.

LIEN: Why were they killed after the war?

MRS DAT: We were the landowners. The peasants fought for the right to own land, and so there were betrayals among brothers, sisters, husbands and wives. They invented the cruellest punishment to eliminate the landowner class. They even shot their own comrades. [*Choking with tears*] The fields were red with blood. Gunshots rang through the night. Finally there was silence. All that was left was a mountain of rotting bodies. Lord Buddha! Let me forget that day, the day they hacked to death my whole family, the day I conceived that child.

> MRS DAT *cries silently. The shadows of* OLD SON *and* HANG *can be seen walking along the riverbank looking up at the black sky. The sounds of wind and gentle waves.*

OLD SON: [*singing*]
Illusion is no longer sacred;
Thousands of lives fell into
The black hole of historical landscape.
I'm a survivor, and becoming a beggar for the past,
Lost among the legendary pain,
Left from the class struggle.
Tears water the tree of the future;
I'm a seeker for tomorrow.
People's hearts resume beating to the same rhythm
To catch up with lost time
And with both hands open to welcome happiness.

LIEN: [*standing up, looking at the ground, trembling with fear*] Mrs Dat, I'll take Hang and we'll go far away. I don't want her to grow up here, where the past can catch up with her. We have to find another life. I wish you well. Goodbye, I must leave you now.

She leaves quickly in the direction of OLD SON *and* HANG. MRS DAT *remains sitting like a stone statue.*

Complete silence, except for the rhythmic movement of MRS DAT*'s arm and the regular sounds of the wooden fish.*

A light flashes. The beating of the wooden fish slows down, then stops. MR THÉ, *dressed in total black, walks in. He stands silently behind* MRS DAT *for a long time.*

MRS DAT: A ghost appears behind my back.

MR THÉ: It's me, Thé.

MRS DAT: Thé died a long time ago. What is left is only a name.

MR THÉ: The name lives, like the bearer of the name. Hmm. People have been raving about the sacredness of Mrs Dat's altar. But all I can see is a dilapidated hut held up by rotting beams.

MRS DAT: If that is all you can see, you don't see Mrs Dat's altar.

MR THÉ: What does it look like?

MRS DAT: It is where the wind blows and the clouds float. It's where people go by, and where the pigs pass.

MR THÉ: Yes, you refer to me as a pig, a goat, a dog. But I'm still a two-legged human being, I still stand upright on this earth.

MRS DAT: That's only the appearance, the soul who dwells inside is another matter.

MR THÉ: Please don't be angry with me. Our lives have taken different roads.

MRS DAT: So what brings you here? What do you want from this skeleton?

MR THÉ: I'm surveying the site for a new construction. Do you want to look at the proposal?

MRS DAT: I haven't opened my eyes for a long time now.

MR THÉ: What have you been praying for, year after year?

MRS DAT: I pray that every life will be allowed to live its full term. I pray that a grain of sand be allowed to be just a grain of sand. That a human being be allowed to be a human being… that's all.

MR THÉ: What are you saying? I don't understand you.

MRS DAT: If everybody understood, life would be less sinful.

MR THÉ: Your son has applied for a housing grant for you and Old Son. I have approved it.

MRS DAT: I no longer give or take anything from this world.

MR THÉ: For your own sake, don't refuse our offer. I'll make sure you'll be able to pray in comfort in your own new house.

MRS DAT: I'd rather die here among my people than leave this peninsula. The earth knows better how to love people than people know how to love one another.

MR THÉ: I'm sorry, Mrs Dat, but—

MRS DAT: Mrs Dat died a long time ago… this is merely an illusion.

MR THÉ: Don't blame me if they force you out when they begin to build [the new construction]. I don't like to see you and Old Son homeless.

MRS DAT: Ideology changes like people change. Only the earth remains constant. Don't worry about me. My spirit will remain here forever even if this old body dies.

MR THÉ: Society changes every minute. If you could be more pragmatic you'd enjoy what is left of your life.

MRS DAT: You know there are thousands of people in this common grave. They had to die because they were born at the wrong time. I want to remain here to pray for their resurrection.

MR THÉ: You are as stubborn as your parents. They kept on denying they were the oppressive class, even at the moment of being axed to death. In any class struggle there are those who survive and those who perish.

MRS DAT: Do you know if you are dead or alive?

MR THÉ: Please! Please stop being… philosophical!

MRS DAT: Can I ask you something?

MR THÉ: Ask anything you like. No matter how difficult a question is, a true Communist will have an answer for it. Do you want to know more about the historical role of the classless revolution in modern society? Or perhaps you'd like to hear about the revolution of information, which is happening right now across the globe? Or maybe you're curious about future life in space?

MRS DAT: Can you tell me how many hairs you have on your head?

MR THÉ: Are you still angry with me for shaving off your hair? An eye for an eye. [*He holds up his leg with the toeless foot and points it at her.*] Surely you haven't forgotten? I was starving, so I climbed the wall of your house to steal some eggs. And to punish me, your father and his cohorts dragged us to the market place and cut off my parents' hands and my toes. Did your father count my toes then? Fair is fair. You've no right to hold a grudge against me. [*He slowly lowers his leg.*] Mrs Dat, please remember—Old Son, you and I were childhood friends.

MRS DAT: The past is only a disappointed dream!

MR THÉ: I'm sorry, but a true Communist has to forget things not worth remembering, so he can concentrate on transforming his pain into revolutionary action.

MRS DAT: Your theory is totally different to your practice. Revolutionary action? No. It was not. You just use that concept to cover your personal rancour.

MR THÉ: I didn't come here to open up old wounds.

MRS DAT: I wonder where we'll meet after we've both left this world and our bones are dug up and destroyed.

MR THÉ: Why do you ask a question like that? There's no point in arranging to meet after we're dead. Say what you want to say now, while we are both still alive. Ah, the fog is thickening. What a dark and cold place!

MRS DAT: The dark and the cold keep people aware of their past, and help them look closely at their present actins.

MR THÉ: Please, don't be so mysterious. Mrs Dat, turn around, look at me and tell me what you want. I haven't seen you for a long time. I want to look at your face again. Have your scars healed?

MRS DAT: Come and have a look, come on, take a look at me.

MR THÉ: [*stumbling in the dark towards* MRS DAT] It's too dark here.

MRS DAT: [*holding a candle in her hand as she turns around, speaking firmly*] I want to look you straight in the face when I tell you to piss off. Now. You're here to betray me. Piss off. I'm staying here to protect the bones.

> *The candle in* MRS DAT*'s hand brightens. The scarf slips off, exposing a completely shaved head and a face covered with long slashing scars. She sits in silence, staring into the empty darkness outside. The lights go off.*

END OF PART ONE

PART TWO

SCENE FOUR

LIFE BEHIND THE WINDOW PANES

At Mr Thé's place. The large room is filled with blue smoke and has a ghostly atmosphere. The dead souls of those killed by Mr Thé appear through the smoke: some without hands, some with nooses around their necks, some with chopsticks poked through their ears, some with open head wounds, some with open chests with blood streaming from them. MR THÉ *looks as if he's being pushed into the room by one of the ghostly appearances. As he falls flat on the floor, we hear the crazy laughter of the dead souls.* MR THÉ *gets up, calmly brushes the dirt off his black suit, and sits down at his desk, staring at the dead souls challenging him.*

MR THÉ: Hey, you homeless dead souls, don't laugh at me too soon. I've never felt powerless in the face of any obstacles. Hey, dead souls, you're always hanging behind me waiting to collect your debts. That bastard wouldn't dare betray me, he always obeys my orders. Hey, wretched souls, don't you laugh at me too soon. [*He holds his toeless foot close to his face.*] My dear toeless foot, when a stranger looks at you, you feel ashamed and humiliated. Thank you for doing the jobs my other senses are no longer capable of.

The dead souls whisper to one another.

What? What are you whispering about! I forbid you to whisper in front of me. My blood is boiling, my insides are twisted. I heard that! So my days are numbered! Is that right? No, no, I can't die yet. You wish I were dead so you can settle the score. Isn't that right? I'm afraid you've got to wait a little longer. I can't die just yet. Go on, keep laughing. I'm not going to die to please you, so don't be so gleeful, you've still got a long time to wait. Piss off! All of you! I can't die yet! [*Screaming at the top of his lungs*] I can't die yet…!

The dead souls disappear with the blue smoke. MR THÉ *puts his head down on the desk. The pale light adds to the ghostly atmosphere of the room.*

A long silence.

The clock chiming brings MR THÉ *out of his dream state.*

I can't die yet. I cannot die yet.

He springs up, goes to the window and looks down on the deserted night street. The wind billows the thin white curtains—they look like funeral hoods flying in the wind. The telephone rings loudly. MR THÉ *picks up the phone.*

[*After a pause*] Let her in.

The large door opens. LIEN *enters. She looks young and beautiful in a sexy see-through dress.* MR THÉ *sits at his desk, still as a ghost. A chair slowly comes out from the dark and stops right in front of* LIEN. *She steps back, stunned.*

Don't be afraid. Please sit down. I was expecting you, but not so late at night.

LIEN: Who told you I was coming?

MR THÉ: [*holding up his toeless foot*] This toeless foot told me. It starts throbbing when someone looks at it. It warned me that you might be hiding under the table the other night, listening to my discussion with your husband.

LIEN: [*dumbfounded*] So that's why you left in a hurry?

MR THÉ: Women should be either beautiful or intelligent. You are both beautiful and intelligent, so you are bound to suffer an unhappy life.

LIEN: [*embarrassed*] I'm sorry. I guess my curiosity was stronger than my manners.

MR THÉ: [*remaining undisturbed*] Oh, I'm not angry with you. All our lives we're filled with desire to know what we shouldn't know. It's a human weakness. But people don't realise that the more you know the more you suffer.

LIEN: I swear to you, I won't tell anyone. It's not in my interest.

MR THÉ: Life has taught me that the best way to keep a promise is never to make a promise. I can see in your eyes that you're in trouble. It's no use trying to hide it. Now tell me, why has your husband ordered you to come here?

LIEN: It's my own decision.

MR THÉ: Your husband is very cunning. Although I think of him as my own son, I have to be cautious in all my dealings with him. It's like using a double-edged sword. I've won and lost many fierce battles in my life. I've never been afraid of the enemy in front of me. But I despise the enemy who stabs me in the back. So, what can an old man like me do for you?

LIEN: I've come to ask for your help. My daughter and I have to get away from this place. You'd never have to worry about my overhearing your plans.

MR THÉ: [*laughing coldly*] But there's nothing secret about it. I'm going to announce the construction project to the media. We want a public opinion poll.

LIEN: A poll on excavating a mass grave?

MR THÉ: [*suddenly standing up, speaking as if giving a speech in front of a large audience*] We are struggling for a free, just and democratic society. The people have the last say. A true Communist is merely a faithful servant of the people. The construction will be a real test for this Revolution. This test will demonstrate to the world that we are democratic. To achieve this great Revolution we have to endure a lot of hardship. I believe we are about to celebrate a great achievement. And you, you want to leave?

LIEN: [*confused*] Are you really going to tell the media what you are planning?

MR THÉ: Honesty is the best way to get what you want in the end!

LIEN: Your confidence is very attractive.

MR THÉ: [*convincingly*] If the people of my generation hadn't been confident, we'd have lost our country by now. [*Softly, maliciously*] Women hide their cunning behind a façade of weakness. Men hide their weakness behind a show of power.

LIEN: [*seductively*] There's nothing weak about you. What I can see in your eyes is loneliness.

MR THÉ: Can loneliness make you hard and cruel?

LIEN: Women are often afraid of cruel men. But they also find them attractive. Cruelty can hide a strength to protect them.

MR THÉ: Do you believe I can protect you?

LIEN: Black suits you.

She goes over and sits on the desk in front of MR THÉ.

If you agree to help me, my body will be at your disposal.

She takes off her clothes. MR THÉ *stands up, slowly puts her clothes back on and walks to the corner.*

MR THÉ: I'll help you get what you want.

LIEN *goes to* MR THÉ *and takes him in her arms.*

LIEN: I like to be fair. And I don't want to be indebted to you.

MR THÉ *moves away and strips off his clothing. His naked body displays multiple hideous scars. His penis is partly sliced off.* LIEN *shudders, steps back and puts her hands over her face.*

How did your body get so badly damaged?

MR THÉ: I was hit by a metal fragment at the battle of Dien Bien Phu. If I'd taken one step forward or one step back, I'd have been able to have a family like any normal man. Alas, one wrong step is all it takes to change your whole life.

LIEN *gently dresses* MR THÉ.

LIEN: I'm sorry.

MR THÉ: [*looking at* LIEN *maliciously*] What would happen if I told your husband about this?

LIEN: I'd be happy for him to know.

MR THÉ: [*laughing triumphantly*] I see. Your husband did order you to come. What does he want from me?

LIEN: He thinks you're keeping something back from him.

MR THÉ: Tragedy begins when people stop trusting one another.

LIEN: Please! Protect me. My husband will kill me. He refused to sign the divorce papers unless I did this for him.

MR THÉ: [*coldly*] Go home. I don't want to interfere in your private life.

LIEN: [*bursting into tears of shame and humiliation*] My private life? What private life! I sacrificed my family to follow the life that Con and you believe in. And now you have the gall to say that you don't want to interfere in my private life. [*Sobbing*] I've come here to demand my life back. Give back my life to me!

MR THÉ: Life is a forward journey. You can never go back. Please, calm down. I know you are under a lot of pressure. Stop crying. I'll help you. Where do you want to go?

LIEN: I don't care as long as I can leave this place forever.

MR THÉ: I'll do whatever you want. I promise. Go home now. The fog's thickening.

> *He finds a red scarf which he places around* LIEN'*s neck.*

There, that'll keep you warm. Next time, don't walk around at night dressed in such flimsy clothes. The street kids might give you a hard time. There! You see! You've reminded me of my duties. Tomorrow I've got to talk to the Education Department about the serious problems we have with young delinquents. Stop crying now, I'll help you get away from this place. Permanently. Take care!

> *Mr Thé's door opens and shuts on its own in order to let* LIEN *out.* MR THÉ *lights up a cigarette and takes a long drag. The smoke hangs in the tense atmosphere. Suddenly he lifts up the telephone.*

I need to arrange an accident involving the won-tan who just left my house. She's wearing a red scarf.

> *Silence and desolation return to the room.* MR THÉ *sits smoking silently, until the voice of* OLD SON *brings him out of his reverie. He listens to the song and again lifts up the handset.*

OLD SON: [*singing*]
> Illusion is no longer sacred;
> Thousands of lives fell into
> The black hole of historical landscape.
> I'm a survivor, and becoming a beggar for the past,
> Lost among the legendary pain,
> Left from the class struggle.
> Tears water the trees of the future;
> I'm a seeker for tomorrow.
> People's hearts resume beating to the same rhythm
> To catch up with lost time
> And with both hands open to welcome happiness.

MR THÉ: Tell that crazy old man who is singing to come up.

> *The large door opens on its own again.* OLD SON *rushes in with joy and swiftly jumps up on the desk. He performs his chant as if he's a professional singer on a stage.* MR THÉ *claps his hands to the beat.*

OLD SON: [*singing*] 'One body has two legs, two arms, two eyes, one trunk and one head. Two bodies have four legs, four arms, four eyes, two trunks and two heads. Three bodies—'

MR THÉ: [*shouting*] Son!

OLD SON: [*stopping singing*] Who is calling my name?

MR THÉ: It's me, Thé, your old friend!

OLD SON: [*looking around, bewildered*] Who is talking to me? Must be a mistake. Friend? The only friends I have are dead.

MR THÉ: [*jumping up on the desk, face to face with* OLD SON] Remember me? Thé!

OLD SON: [*jumping off the desk, looking at* MR THÉ, *frightened*] Which Thé?

MR THÉ: [*balancing himself on one leg, holding up the toeless foot*] Thé, whose toes were cut off by a rich landowner in the middle of the market. Remember me?

OLD SON: [*jumping up and down with joy*] Ah—Thé! It is you. How could I forget you?

> *He jumps up on the desk and embraces* MR THÉ. *Unexpectedly he gives* MR THÉ *a push.* MR THÉ *falls off the desk.*

I'm so happy to see you again.

MR THÉ: Ouch, that hurts.

OLD SON: [*laughing heartily*] The more one falls, the wiser one gets. Let's look at you.

MR THÉ: You realise we are no longer children.

OLD SON: I feel like giving you a big bite to express my joy over meeting you again.

> OLD SON *jumps off the desk and tries to give* MR THÉ *a big bite.* MR THÉ *runs away. They chase each other around the room until* OLD SON *catches up with* MR THÉ, *grabs him and looks at him closely, wild with excitement.*

So many years and you haven't changed much. The same ill-bred look of a peasant. And how have you been? Still eating three meals a day? Still peeing and poohing regularly? You took like you can afford a daily change of clothes, too?

MR THÉ: Well, look at me—what do you think? And what are you doing? Wandering around late at night on your own?

OLD SON: I'm looking for the future.

MR THÉ: Have you found it?

OLD SON: [*opening up his hands*] I wasted my whole life before I realised that the future is in my own hands.

> *He smells* MR THÉ.

Gosh, you stink. The smelt of deceit. Invisible, intangible deceit, but it still stinks.

MR THÉ: You're teasing me. Remember how you used to tease me when we were children flying kites on the riverbank?

OLD SON: How could I forget it? We both chased after Miss Dat, without success. I remember during the Land Reform Movement, they chose you to wear the leader armband. You looked so proud—you killed everyone in her family with your own hoe, and yet you weren't satisfied. Your red armband and your hoe heralded death wherever you went. How many more victims have been added to your victory list?

MR THÉ: We haven't seen each other for a long time. Why all this talk of death? Hey, Son, what happened to our lives? How come we only have cruel things to say to each other? Don't you have any happy memories of me?

OLD SON: Ah yes, you offered me boiled pig's head with fish and ginger sauce. I remember it very clearly. I'd hardly swallowed the first mouthful before you had me thrown into prison for siding with the oppressive Landowner. When I was in prison, the guards tried to push chopsticks through my ears while I was asleep. You see, I refused to massage them and carry water for their dirty bums! Since then I've always slept with my hands covering my ears—like this. It's become a bad habit. [*Laughing maniacally, singing*] 'One body has two legs, two arms, two eyes, one trunk and one head. Two bodies have four legs, four arms, four eyes, two trunks and two heads. Three bodies—'

MR THÉ: Please stop singing. Let's talk about something else. What's all this singing about anyway? What do you do for a living? You must be doing all right to spend your days singing away so happily.

OLD SON: I plant trees for the lives of those who are dead, and dig graves for those who should have died a long time ago. Somehow they manage to stay alive.

MR THÉ: Could you dig a grave for me? I've no relatives left. No one to dig my grave.

OLD SON: You should dig your own grave. Why not do it now while you can? How about I lend you my shovel and give you a few tips how to do it? I'll only trust you after you're dead. As long as you're alive, I have to keep a close watch on you.

MR THÉ: What can you possibly do for me once I'm dead?

OLD SON: When people die, they leave behind a number of things they can't do themselves. I know for sure I'll have to do two things for you. I have to bury you and make sure your grave is well kept. Then I have to pray for your soul to be reborn in a better person than you are now.

MR THÉ: [*reaching out to hold* OLD SON*'s hand*] I don't understand. You're cursing me, yet you want to look after me when I die? I realise you think I'm an ill-bred renegade. But I want you to know one thing—I was not born a bad person. Our mothers give birth to us, and life keeps pushing us along. All my life all I've tried to do is change our unfortunate fate. Is that a crime?

OLD SON: No. It's just that there's a difference between theory and practice. Some actions can only be corrected by death. In death, there is a small joy, the chance to be reborn. That's why I'll only look after you when you die.

MR THÉ: [*angrily*] I didn't invite you here to lecture me on how to live. I'm not in a hurry to die, so don't worry about looking after my grave and burning incense to pray for my soul. I've got to live till I can see with my own eyes that my revolutionary ideals have become a reality.

OLD SON: [*laughing crazily*] You are as bad as before. But I promise you, even if you were ten times worse, I'd still look after your grave and pray for your soul. I owe that to our friendship.

MR THÉ: [*roaring like a wounded beast*] Oh, fuck our friendship! Son, you haven't changed a bit. The same poor, hungry and dirty old bag of bones. After all these years you still haven't woken up to reality. I'm warning you, if you keep loitering near my house singing this stupid nonsense, you might die before me. The difference is, I'll piss on your grave. Now get out.

> *A long silence.* OLD SON *remains as still as a statue. The lights go off.*

SCENE FIVE

THE DAY WHEN THE LANDLESS PEASANTS RISE UP

Con's dining room. A small altar hangs from the wall with a photo of LIEN *in the middle. The room is filled with incense and lit by altar candles.* MRS DAT *sits immobile at the dining table. A scarf completely covers her head and her face except for the eyes.* CON *sits opposite her showing no emotion. A tense silence. From the smoke,* LIEN'*s dead soul, in floating white garments, appears and disappears.*

CON: Do you realise that, because of you, I've been demoted? In the most polite way, of course. What did you say to my boss when he came to visit?

MRS DAT: I talked about the good and the bad old days, when we were friends.

CON: You're old, it'd be best if you were to die. The longer you live the more trouble you cause me, and the more spoiled your granddaughter becomes, and I'll go crazy and kill you.

MRS DAT: Don't worry. I don't think I want to live much longer. I'm only here to light some incense and say a prayer for your dead wife. She was, after all, my daughter-in-law.

CON: My wife was stupid and that's why she died. Death is final. Why bother about prayers? Tell me, why are you trying to block my plans? If you don't tell me, I'll kill you, kill myself, and kill my daughter, right now!

MRS DAT: Please, Con, my son, don't do that. You can kill me if you want. You can kill yourself if you want. But don't kill your daughter. She's the future of this land.

CON: Fuck the future! I want to know the past first. How can we go to the future if we don't know the past? Tell me! Now!

> LIEN'S SOUL *steps out from the smoke, from the world of the dead souls.*

LIEN'S SOUL: Tell him. If only I could be alive again for just a few minutes, to tell you that death is not final. Only after we die can we understand the meaning of each day of our lives. Your mother has to suffer all her life for you, Con. I wish I could tell you that too. Mrs Dat! Tell him the story that changed your life, the story of your long suffering. Tell him. Tell him. Tell him.

> *As* MRS DAT *begins her story, voices of the dead souls sing from under the ground.*

MRS DAT: Mr Thé, Old Son and I grew up together in this village. My family forbade me to play with them because they were from poor peasant families. That year, the rice crop failed, and all the peasants were starving. Mr Thé climbed over the wall of my house to steal some eggs. He was caught red-handed by your grandfather and the village guards. They took him and every member of his family to the market place for punishment. Some had their toes cut off, some had their hands cut off. I failed to stop it. Since then the hatred for my family… [*Choking with tears*] War followed. Mr Thé volunteered to fight against the French. He fought at the battle of Dien Bien Phu. On Victory Day he returned to the village a hero, his uniforms covered with medals. Crowds of people gathered to stare at his amazing wounds. Each wound and each medal represented a victory. There was a rumour that one of his victories had made him incapable of having children. That same year they launched the Land Reform Movement. Its aim was to eliminate the landowners and redistribute their lands to the peasants. Mr Thé was elected Leader of the Movement for this region. My family knew that the day for his revenge had come. But no one could predict how barbaric his revenge was going to be… You weren't even born yet.

> *Suddenly the lights go off. From the darkness we hear the screaming sounds of peasants accusing their landlords. Gunshots come from all directions. The ground rumbles under the feet of thousands of peasants searching for landowners. Lights from a burning torch show up the tortured victims.*

FEMALE PEASANT: Shot him right in the belly! I worked for his family. He used to steal half of my lunch and then beat me senseless.

MALE PEASANT: Come on, everyone, stone him! He used to feel up my wife and make her sit up all night fanning off mosquitoes and stroking his back.

YOUNG MALE PEASANT: Let's throw shit on her head. She never paid me for my work.

FEMALE PEASANT: Let's burn him alive! He tied my husband to a tree and made him watch while they raped me.

> *The sounds of stones being thrown onto the tortured.* MR THÉ *walks in, an overbearing young man wearing a red armband with writing in yellow: 'Regional Leader, Land Reform Movement'. He carries a bloody hoe in one hand, in the other a plate of boiled pig's head still steaming hot.* SON *follows, carrying pen and papers. Echoes of the painful screams of victims being tortured.*

MR THÉ: Nice meat! Have some while it's still hot.

SON: I'm admiring your armband.

MR THÉ: Impressive?

SON: Very impressive, especially when you think of all the times we were bullied by the rich boys.

MR THÉ: Don't worry. I'll fix them. I'll dig up their ancestral graves. I'll push their faces into the muddy field and drown them, that'll wipe the grin off their faces. How dare they mock our poverty. Here, have some meat while it's still hot. Umm! Excellent meat, this. Especially with fish and ginger sauce.

SON: When we were hired labourers, we ate with our fingers, and now we use chopsticks to pick up pieces of steaming hot meat. I can't tell you how exhilarated it makes me feel. [*Pause.*] But why have you gone quiet?

MR THÉ: I feel sorry for my parents. After their hands were cut off, they had to eat like dogs, dipping their faces in the bowl. They couldn't bear the humiliation, they ended up killing themselves.

SON: I thought you'd already taken revenge on the people who chopped off your parents' hands?

MR THÉ: Yes, I killed every single one of them with my own hoe, and yet I don't feel any less hatred. [*He picks up a piece of meat, holding it up in front of him as an offering.*] Dear Father and Mother—what about you, are you happy?

SON: I'll write a play in praise of your victorious achievements in the Land Reform Movement. Then you'll be awarded more medals.

MR THÉ: I know you're a good playwright. I'd love a few great plays about this magnificent Revolution. If you need anything at all, just ask.

A young PEASANT *enters quickly, holding a thick book, clicking his bare feet respectfully together.* MR THÉ *glares at him.*

PEASANT: I'd like to report to our Leader that today our Unit surpassed the target set by the Revolutionary Committee. We hanged twenty-seven oppressive landowners, shot thirty-six wealthy traders, drowned forty-five suspects who were accused of bullying innocent people. Also, Party members assisted other peasants to stone to death fifty-four people who were suspected of being spies for the rich. And here are a couple of execution forms for you to sign. It concerns two people I just arrested: Dong from the Lower Hamlet and Doai from the Upper Hamlet. Please sign them so we can execute the sentence.

MR THÉ: The nose part of the pig's head looks rather crunchy! Have some more, it is still hot.

He pulls out a biro from his shirt pocket, clicks it and signs the forms which the young man hands to him.

We're enjoying our meat and you interrupt me for a signature!

SON: [*grabbing the young man's hand*] Wait! What are their crimes? Thé, you can't sign a death warrant without knowing what they're guilty of.

PEASANT: The Land Reform Unit found a pottery vase hidden at Dong's place, and two stainless steel bowls at Doai's place. Obviously they've exploited the People. And yet, when being arrested, they still cried out: 'Long live the Revolution.' If they weren't traitors, how could they own pottery vases and stainless steel bowls?

SON: Thé, you must reconsider. During the struggle, those two offered plenty of rice and money to the Revolution. You can't kill them for owning a pottery vase and a couple of steel bowls!

MR THÉ: [*indifferently*] Here, have another piece of meat, eat up!

SON: [*taking the meat, slowly chewing it*] Please reconsider. We'll destroy the aim of the Revolution if we kill the wrong people.

MR THÉ: [*screaming at the top of his voice unexpectedly, the piece of meat on his chopsticks nearly falling off*] Guard!

PEASANT: [*clicking his bare heels together*] Yes, sir!

MR THÉ: Throw him in jail now.

SON: [*unbelieving*] Thé, what do you think you're doing? We grew up together in poverty. How can you possibly think I'm your enemy?

MR THÉ: [*coldly*] Exploitation of the People is a crime against the People.

SON: Thé! I'm not your enemy! You're wrong!

> *The young* PEASANT *takes* SON *away, to the sounds of the People's uprising.* MR THÉ *sits indifferently, carefully carving some more meat for himself. The young* PEASANT *returns with a young girl with very long hair, young* MISS DAT. *He pushes her to the floor in front of* MR THÉ.

PEASANT: Sir, I found her hiding in a stack of straw at the end of the village. I recognise her. It was her father who cut off your toes. I bring her to you so you can punish her yourself.

MISS DAT: Thé, you have killed every member of my family. Please let me go. Don't you remember, I tried to stop my father punishing you and your family. We used to be good friends. Please let me live.

MR THÉ: [*beckoning*] Come here! No, don't be afraid, I'm not going to kill you.

> *She crawls over to* MR THÉ *who stretches out his toeless foot. She looks at him, frightened.*

So you want me to spare your life? Lick my foot!

MISS DAT: Please. I beg you, don't humiliate me like this!

MR THÉ: [*roaring*] That's exactly how I begged your father!

MISS DAT: I'll never lick your foot. If you want to kill me, kill me!

MR THÉ: Oh no, I don't want to kill you. I want you to exist in a living Hell. Your father left me scarred for life, and now I'm going to give you scars you'll live with forever!

> *Suddenly* MR THÉ *grabs her hair, takes out his knife and shaves it off. Then he holds her head between his leg and slashes her face indiscriminately. The girl covers her bloody face with her hands and rolls around in pain. The young* PEASANT *laughs approvingly and happily jumps up and down.*

PEASANT: That serves you right. Exploiter!

MR THÉ: [*pointing the bloody knife at the* PEASANT] Take off your clothes. Rape her for me.

PEASANT: Please, sir, I leave that pleasure to you, sir.

MR THÉ: [*roaring*] If I were capable of doing it, I wouldn't ask you! I order you to do it in the name of the Revolution. Do it!

PEASANT: Yes, sir, I'll obey your order.

> MR THÉ *sits indifferently, continuing to eat his meat. The young* PEASANT *takes off his trousers and rapes the young girl, who struggles desperately until she passes out from exhaustion. The* PEASANT *puts back his trousers, walks to* MR THÉ *and clicks his bare heels together.*

Sir, I have done my duty.

MR THÉ: [*with his mouth full of food*] What duty did I give you?

PEASANT: [*bewildered*] I raped her as you ordered!

MR THÉ: [*picking up bundles of the young girl's long hair and walking over to the young* PEASANT] I never ordered you to rape the girl.

> *He places the bundle of long hair around the* PEASANT's *neck and starts strangling him.*

You'll die for this. Anything to say?

PEASANT: [*struggling to scream*] What crime did I commit? Why do you want to kill me? I only obeyed your order.

MR THÉ: You have to die because you obeyed my order.

> MR THÉ *tightens the hair bundle. The young* PEASANT *stops breathing, the body falls to the floor.* MR THÉ *stands still and stares into the night. Torchlight flares up every now and then to light up the darkness. He walks around aimlessly. The girl slowly sits up, her hands clasped in front of her naked torso.*

MISS DAT: Please, Lord Buddha, if I were to be reborn, don't make me be a human being again, let me be a plant, a leaf or a flower. Please.

MR THÉ: In our class struggle, achievement is measured by body count. It's better to kill an innocent than miss an enemy. The more you kill, the more chance you have of surviving. For the sake of our friendship, I want to tell you something I've been keeping to myself. I've realised for a long time now that what I've been ordered to do goes against the revolutionary ideal. But I've got to keep my mouth shut or my head will be cracked open by someone else's hoe. To survive in this deadly climate, you have to be two-faced. Don't think I want to be reborn a human being again. No, never, never again.

MR THÉ *looks up to the dark sky as if to stop his tears from rolling down.*

A long silence.

Darkness slowly invades the room. The last of the pale moon is completely covered by dark clouds. The lights return to Con's dining room where LIEN'S SOUL, MRS DAT *and* CON *all sit still like statues. Sounds of people being tortured linger on in the room. They slowly fade away to complete silence. Everything is completely still behind the swirling smoke of the incense.*

A long silence. Long silence. Long silence.

The lights go off.

SCENE SIX

THE FIRE WILL BE BURNING FOREVER

A riverbank dimly lit by the lamps of the fishermen's boats anchored in the fast flowing river. As the night progresses the noises diminish, except for the regular sound of waves against the riverbank and the rustle of trees in the light wind. Two shadows appear. CON *and* MR THÉ *enter.* CON *suddenly pulls his gun and points it at* MR THÉ'*s head.*

MR THÉ: I know why you asked me to come here in the middle of the night. I know I'll die tonight. But you'd be stupid to pull the trigger.

CON: It's going to give me enormous pleasure to kill you with the very gun you gave me.

MR THÉ: [*laughing drily*] Ah! If you want to live a little longer, you should think twice about shooting me. If I die, you wouldn't escape death either. You really should make a wiser decision to match your reputation of being a clever overseas-trained politician.

CON: You've got to die.

MR THÉ: Do you think I'm afraid to die? No. Not at all.

CON: I've trusted you and believed in you all my life. But you killed my father, slashed my mother's face and had my wife executed!

MR THÉ: Don't be so quick to pass judgement. Just remember, without me you're nothing. A poverty-stricken, powerless bastard. I gave you everything, even the gun you're pointing at me.

CON: Fuck you. Fuck you! I'd throw all of it back in your face in exchange for my old life.

MR THÉ: Ah! Even the life you thought yours, I gave you. If I hadn't ordered the rape of your mother, you wouldn't exist. That's why I've been protecting you as if you were my own son. You should be grateful to me.

CON: Don't build up any hopes you'll live after tonight.

MR THÉ: I don't want to beg you for forgiveness. But I don't want you to die for my murder either. Killing people is easy. To be able to live after the killing is much more difficult.

CON: Choose your own way to die!

MR THÉ: That's exactly what I'd expect from an intelligent man like you. It's a fair exchange for what I've given you. I don't want anyone to suffer for my death. And I don't want anyone to know how I died. I want to leave this world. It's got nothing left to offer me.

CON: It's nearly day break. We have very little time left. Choose!

MR THÉ: Put your gun away. Sit down and watch me dig my own grave. When it's done, all you have to do is fill it with soil.

CON: [*bewildered*] Do you want me to bury you alive?

MR THÉ: That would be best for both of us. You won't have to pay for killing me, and I'll choose how to die, just as I chose how to live. Keep the gun. We shared many things in life, now let me have my own death.

CON: [*putting the gun in his pocket*] Shut up and start digging.

> MR THÉ *starts digging his own grave enthusiastically, with* CON *following every movement. The lamps from the fishing boats flicker as the boats bob up and down. The sound of the wind rustling in the trees mingles with the singing of the boatmen.*

Do you have any regrets?

MR THÉ: [*stopping digging, wiping the sweat from his face with his hand*] I believe I've lived my life as it was meant to be.

CON: Do you consider your life happy or unhappy?

MR THÉ: [*continuing to dig*] I feel happy for having lived, and I feel unhappy for having been born. Come and tell me if this is deep enough.

CON: It's your grave.

MR THÉ: That's the spirit. Everyone's responsible for their own life and death. How fortunate that the soil is so soft, I'm lucky that my corpse will be nourished by this rich silt.

> MR THÉ *continues digging.* CON *stands at the edge looking down.* MR THÉ *looks up at him.*
>
> *A long silence.*
>
> MR THÉ *smiles, a crazy look on his face. Suddenly, he bursts out laughing, and starts dancing and singing.*

[*Singing loudly*] 'One body has two legs, two ears, two eyes, one trunk and one head; two bodies have four legs, four ears, four eyes, two trunks, two heads la, la, la. Three bodies have six legs…'

> CON *looks around worriedly. He lifts up the shovel and quickly starts throwing soil into the grave.* MR THÉ *keeps on singing and dancing crazily.*
>
> *The hole is slowly filled up until the singing is finally silenced. One of* MR THÉ*'s arms can be seen twitching, trying to hold onto life.* CON *continues shovelling.* MR THÉ*'s arm flops down and disappears.* CON *keeps throwing soil on the grave until footsteps approach and a lit torch appears. He quickly moves to a dark corner.* SON *and* HANG *enter.*

OLD SON: I'm certain I could hear someone sing.

HANG: Come on! You're hearing things again. No one comes here at this time of night.

OLD SON: I suspect someone might come to steal the new seedlings we planted this afternoon. [*He sits down and tends to the seedlings.*] To plant a tree in the earth is like giving birth to a new life. A tree is like a person. The tree only produces nice sweet fruits if it's well cared for. People can only enjoy a good happy life if they're suitably nurtured.

HANG: You speak beautifully, like poetry. I prefer this to your stories about death and ghosts. They scare me.

OLD SON: Remember, the secret I told you this afternoon is between you and me only.

HANG: [*chuckling with her hands over her mouth*] You're such a good actor! You fooled everybody! [*She sees the shovel and the new pile of dirt.*] Old Son, look! Someone was here, digging.

OLD SON: [*running over*] Looks like it, doesn't it? [*Holding up the torch*] You have good eyes. Is that someone hiding over there, in the dark?

HANG: [*straining her eyes*] Yes, it's a man.

OLD SON: [*shouting*] Who is there?

CON: [*walking out from the dark*] It's only me, don't make such a racket!

HANG: [*recognising* CON, *immediately hiding herself*] Old Son! It's my father. He's looking for me. Please tell him I don't want to go home. I want to stay here. I'm afraid of him.

OLD SON: [*looking at* CON, *frightened*] I didn't know you were here…

CON: Don't be afraid. I'm not going to do anything to you.

OLD SON: [*standing in front of* HANG *in order to hide her*] What are you doing here at this hour of the night? Why have you been digging?

CON: I just buried my life belief here.

OLD SON: No wonder you look so sad. Do you want me to plant a new seedling on the grave of your life belief?

CON: A life belief also possesses a soul. All departed souls need a proper send-off. Yes, please plant a tree on it for me.

OLD SON: What do you want as an epitaph?

CON: 'A Graveyard for the Living'.

OLD SON: That's sad. I'll plant a tree in the hope that it'll help make your life happier.

CON: Has your life been happy?

OLD SON: Now that I've nearly lived out my life, I'm beginning to feel happy. And you, is your life a happy one?

CON: No. But I feel a little joy from the beginning of your happiness. [*Pause.*] You're only playing mad, aren't you?

HANG: [*jumping out from behind* OLD SON] Old Son isn't crazy. Those who think he is are really the mad ones. His madness has saved his life a few times. If they didn't think he was a crazy old fool, he wouldn't have got out of prison, and perhaps they'd have pushed chopsticks through his ears to kill him a long time ago.

OLD SON: Hang! You promised not to reveal my secret.

HANG: I'm sorry, Old Son. He thought he knew everything but really he knows nothing.

CON: Hang, my daughter, please come home, I'll look after you.

HANG: No, never. I'll never come back. You scare me. I'll stay here with Grandma and Old Son and take care of the peninsula.

CON: Please come home, I'll do everything to be a good father to you.

HANG: I don't believe you're capable of change.

CON: [*raising his voice*] I'll force you home.

HANG: [*staying away from her father*] I'm not coming. I don't trust you.

> HANG *cries loudly in* OLD SON*'s arms.* CON *sits powerless and dejected.* MRS DAT *quietly enters.*

MRS DAT: What's happened, why is my granddaughter crying?

CON: [*jumping up and roaring with anger*] What lies have you been telling my daughter? She is scared of me. She doesn't want to come near me!

MRS DAT: [*clasping herself, trembling*] Don't shout at me. You know your shouting causes pain in my heart.

CON: [*roaring even louder*] My daughter will never trust me again!

MRS DAT: [*lowering herself to the ground*] All I can tell her is that one should love one's parents. I don't know why she no longer trusts you. Children these day mature more quickly. They create their own faith.

CON: Why was I born to suffer this life?

MRS DAT: I wish he'd killed me that day so you wouldn't have been born. I don't mind if you blame me for all your sufferings. All I want is for you to be at peace with yourself.

CON: Why didn't you tell me everything earlier?

MRS DAT: What would your life have been, knowing you were the result of a rape? I didn't want you to know. I tried to keep your heart untainted; not full of hurt and pain.

CON: [*unhappily*] But you didn't succeed, did you? How could you? Life's dirty and full of deceit. The only way to remain untainted is never to be born. Perhaps if you'd told me about it earlier, life might've been a bit different. But now everything's finished for me. I'm glad you told me about my origins. I'm grateful to you for giving me a life, and I curse you for it. Goodbye, my mother.

MRS DAT: Where can you go?

CON: I don't know—

> CON *leaves slowly, totally dejected.*
>
> *A long silence.*
>
> *Suddenly the sound of a loud gunshot is heard from the river bank.* MRS DAT *clasps herself as if to stop her heart from exploding*

with the pain of a mother who has just lost her son. SON *and* HANG *run to her side.*

MRS DAT: There are millions of people in this land but I only have one son. Please forgive me that I wasn't able to offer him the life he wished for.

HANG: [*bursting into tears*] Grandma, my mother is dead, and my father is dead. I only have you and Old Son left. Please don't leave me on my own, please promise me that you won't die. Old Son, you've got to promise me, too, that you won't die.

OLD SON: Stop crying, my little one. I promise you. I'll live as long as I possibly can. I must live so you and I can grow more trees on this peninsula. I must live so I can see you paint.

HANG: Old Son has made his promise. Grandma, you have to promise me as well.

MRS DAT: I promise you, I'll live as long as I can keep myself alive. I'll tell you a story that'll make you feet confident about your future.

HANG: What story are you going to tell me?

MRS DAT: Once upon a time, on a peninsula next to a fast flowing river…

OLD SON: … where there are rows of green trees, and voices of boatmen singing…

HANG: [*with enthusiasm*] … with a warm fire that lights up the darkness of the night.

MRS DAT: Life changes, always, but the fire will keep on burning forever.

Dawn is breaking. The sky seems higher and bluer. The red sun is slowly rising on the horizon behind the sails of the fishing boats. Waves are tapping against the riverbank and the boatmen are singing. The flow of the river carries along the rich silt. The river carries with it the hearts of many people. The river carries so many dreams going to the sea.

THE END